"Faith flows naturally from the heart of a surrendered believer. While faith does not come from the mind, the renewed mind enhances faith as a lifestyle. Here is where James Goll's *A Radical Faith* comes into play. On these pages, James deals meticulously with truths that help set our hearts and minds in proper alignment with the heart of God—the true source of all faith. Jesus told us that the truth will set us free. In *A Radical Faith*, readers will discover the freedom to believe God with all their hearts. I recommend this book for the new and seasoned believer alike."

Bill Johnson, senior leader, Bethel Church, Redding, California; author, *When Heaven Invades Earth* and *Face to Face with God*

"James Goll is a man of the Word and a man of the Spirit. In his newest book, his love for the Word of God is both evident and inspiring. If you are a new believer, this volume will guide you through the foundational tenets of your newfound faith and will ground you in the beliefs you need for a lifetime. If you are a mature believer, read this book as a fresh reminder of the truths you hold so dear!"

Jane Hansen Hoyt, president/CEO, Aglow International

"This is a handbook to ensure our destiny in the Kingdom of God. Whether you have found Jesus recently or have a long legacy in the faith, it is worth perusing the important principles James Goll discusses. Champions in every field need a back-to-basics retreat in order to shore up the cracks in their foundations. In this same spirit, I categorically declare that this book delivers spiritual 'caulk' for the Christian walk. James Goll reminds us that we cannot take anything on this earth for granted. Let's make sure we are grounded!"

Harry R. Jackson Jr., senior pastor, Hope Christian Church (Washington, D.C., area); founder and president, High Impact Leadership Coalition

"Without faith it is impossible to please God. Be discipled by James Goll through the pages of this outstanding book and be equipped to have an unshakable foundation in Jesus Christ. James has exemplified honorary faith and lives what he is teaching. May this book encourage you as much as James's life has impacted me."

Ché Ahn, senior pastor, HROCK Church, Pasadena, California; international chancellor, Wagner Leadership Institute; president, Harvest International Ministry

"James Goll's *A Radical Faith* more than lives up to its title. A useful resource for all believers, this book amounts to a fascinating personal catechism based on the author's rich experiences in the faith. I highly recommend it."

Vinson Synan, dean emeritus, Regent University School of Divinity

"In a day when many want a quick fix, James Goll has confronted the reader with the folly of shortcuts and of taking the Word of God lightly. James stresses getting to one's roots before one can grow."

R. T. Kendall, former minister, Westminster Chapel, London; from the foreword of *A Radical Faith*

A RADICAL FAITH STUDY GUIDE

A
RADICAL
FAITH

ESSENTIALS FOR SPIRIT-FILLED BELIEVERS

STUDY GUIDE

JAMES W. GOLL

Chosen
a division of Baker Publishing Group
Minneapolis, Minnesota

© 2011 by James W. Goll

Published by Chosen Books
11400 Hampshire Avenue South
Bloomington, MN 55438
www.chosenbooks.com

Chosen Books is a division of
Baker Publishing Group, Grand Rapids, Michigan.
Printed in the United States of America

ISBN 978-0-8007-9509-2

Cover design by Dan Pitts

11   12   13   14   15   16   17   7   6   5   4   3   2   1

This study guide is dedicated to all believers who wish to be consecrated disciples of the Lord Jesus Christ and who wish to help others become disciples as well. Grounded on these scriptural truths and elementary principles of Christ, I want you to be able to build a skyscraper for Jesus. May this study guide anchor you in the Lordship of Jesus, who is not only your Savior but also your Lord. God bless you as you read and study these truths and pass them on to others for His name's sake.

" . . . laying again the foundation of repentance from dead works and of faith toward God, of the doctrine of baptisms, of laying on of hands, of resurrection of the dead, and of eternal judgment. . . ."

Hebrews 6:1–2

A Radical Faith Study Guide

This study guide has been prepared with your individual, small group or training center needs in mind. The lessons coordinate with the chapters of the book, *A Radical Faith*, also published by Chosen Books.

At the end of each lesson, you will find Reflection Questions to help you review what you have studied.

CDs and DVDs that match each lesson can be purchased from Encounters Network (contact information at the end of the study guide).

CONTENTS

FOREWORD

What an amazing idea! Though I am sure it has been done before, I cannot remember seeing it done so profoundly simply and simply profound. I am speaking of James Goll's work, *A Radical Faith*. There is an exceedingly healthy trend among us toward getting back to the basics, and James provides us with a new meaning of such.

I am talking about a reexamination, restatement and re-celebration of the verities of our faith: the Word of God, the Trinity, salvation, repentance, grace, faith, baptisms, resurrection and judgment, among others. Nothing will serve to cause our faith to escalate, our hope to crystallize, our praises to rise like a fresh look at all that is ours here and hereafter.

James Goll has a way of reducing every major tenet of our great belief system into understandable terms, inspirational concepts and applicable conclusions. I can see anyone profiting who will work through the questions and answers and meditate on these items we so often take for granted.

This work breathes life and is vintage James Goll. It rises out of his walk through the dark valley that none of us chooses to walk. But God in His infinite wisdom and providence walks with us through these heavenly appointments to teach us to join Him in knowing more deeply the God of all comforts. And all these truths, so well reintroduced, will escort us all through life and into eternity!

I recommend this fine work excitedly and enthusiastically. Thanks, James!

—Jack Taylor, president, Dimensions Ministries

PREFACE

Built on Nothing Less

When you decide to design and build a house, you need to get the best building materials you can find. Thus supplied, you must start by constructing a firm foundation. The foundation is all-important to your effort. Without a firm foundation, you will be sunk, possibly quite literally.

This commonsense principle applies to houses of all sizes and descriptions—and by extension even the most basic "house" of all—the human body that houses your spirit and soul. God wants to help you build a stable, successful Christian life that is firmly rooted in Jesus Christ. He will provide you with all of the building materials as well as detailed building and maintenance instructions. Because you have given Him your assent, He Himself *is* the foundation, and He will see to it that you and anybody else who names His name will enjoy eternal-lifetime-guaranteed success.

That is the ideal, anyway. But even with everything that has been made available to you as regards His construction supplies and expert advice, how can you be sure that you have selected the very best foundation-building materials? What if, back when you first became a Christian, somebody sold you a bill of goods? What if your foundation has been laid poorly? Is it too late to rebuild?

The writer of the biblical letter to the Hebrews gave us a brief listing of the components of a firm foundation when he wrote the words that I have chosen as the theme Scripture of this study:

> Leaving the discussion of the elementary principles of Christ, let us go on to perfection, not laying again the foundation of repentance from dead works and of faith toward God, of the doctrine of baptisms, of laying on of hands, of resurrection of the dead, and of eternal judgment.
>
> Hebrews 6:1–2

The writer assumed that the believers he was addressing were mature enough to leave behind the discussion of such elementary principles as these. Fair enough for those ancient Hebrews. But for most of us, a review brings tangible benefits.

That is what I intend to do for you in this study guide and its companion book, *A Radical Faith*. Here I have summarized, with abundant biblical support, the basics of the Christian faith. In essence, this is a Bible study with the theme of the enduring fundamentals of the faith that must be built into the foundation of every mature Christian.

For some of you, this study guide will be a simple review. For others, especially those of you who are new to the faith or whose exposure to foundational truths has been deficient or partial, it will provide a vital shoring up of the basis for your new life in Christ. For all believers, this extended study can furnish a framework for personal Christian life as well as an outline for mentoring others.

All of us dwell in an environment that is hostile to our outposts of the heavenly Kingdom, and we must battle against an enemy who wants nothing more than to undermine our foundations. King David wrote, "If the foundations are destroyed, what can the righteous do?" (Psalm 11:3). To keep erosion from happening, we must constantly renew our minds with the truth of God's Word, reinforcing the basic underpinnings so that we can continue to grow and bear fruit for the Kingdom of God.

God's blueprints and His master plan for building the house of your life are contained in the Bible. He Himself is the Architect and the Builder. In this study guide, I have provided twelve lessons on twelve distinct, foundational aspects of a believer's life. These match the chapters of *A Radical Faith*.

Other teachers may wish I had covered more (or fewer) topics in greater (or less) detail. But I feel that these particular topics, taken from that verse in Hebrews quoted above and from other important verses, do cover the basics. As I have organized this material and reworked it, I have been newly motivated to dedicate myself afresh to the Master Builder's excellent construction process, and I trust that the same thing will happen for you.

David's son Solomon wrote, "Unless the LORD builds the house, they labor in vain who build it" (Psalm 127:1). May the Holy Spirit guide you through this study and help you establish a foundation that is firmer than ever, for the glory of Jesus Christ.

In the words of the old hymn: "My hope is built on nothing less/ Than Jesus' blood and righteousness. . . . On Christ the solid Rock I stand,/ All other ground is sinking sand."[1]*

James W. Goll

---

1. * First two lines from the first stanza and refrain of the hymn, "My Hope Is Built," by Edward Mote (lyrics in the public domain).

ACKNOWLEDGMENTS

Thanks goes to all the teachers, pastors, leaders and mentors in my life who have grounded me in the Word of God and in the ways of the Holy Spirit. A huge thanks, first and foremost, goes to the late Bible teacher Derek Prince, whose materials I devoured in the early years of my Christian formation. Derek's fingerprints are all over this study guide.

Special thanks also goes to Jim Croft, the late Ernest J. Gruen, Mahesh Chavda, David Altschul, Geoff Buck, Mike Bickle and many others for walking with me over the years—teaching me, leading me and walking by my side. As pastors and leaders in the Body of Christ, your influence has made an imprint on my life. Thank you for giving to me so that I could freely give to others!

A bucketful of thanks belongs to the faithful team that made this project possible. My writing assistant, Kathy Deering, has been a godsend to me for the past several years and has again been marvelously instrumental in this writing project. You are just excellent and brilliant! I thank the Lord for Chosen Books and for Jane Campbell, who continues to believe and invest in me. Your integrity shines brightly. The board of directors and staff of Encounters Network has been a constant source of encouragement to me. Our network prayer warriors and ministry partners consistently hold up my hands during every writing project. Indeed, they are the unseen force behind the scenes. Thank you, each and every one.

With Gratitude,
Dr. James W. Goll

LESSON 1

THE FOUNDATION FOR ALL BELIEVERS

I. The Believer's Life Compared to a Building

A. In the language of the Bible, the believer's life is compared to a well-built structure constructed on a firm foundation, and the believer is expected to be active in the building process.

> You, beloved, building yourselves up on your most holy faith, praying in the Holy Spirit.
>
> Jude 20

B. In the natural realm, the most important feature of any structure is its foundation. The foundation sets the limit to the weight and size of the building erected upon it. A small or weak foundation can support only a small building. In like manner, a deep or strong foundation can support a large building. The same is true of our spiritual lives.

> We are God's fellow workers; . . . you are God's building. According to the grace of God which was given to me, as a wise master builder I have laid the foundation, and another builds on it. But let each one take heed how he builds on it.
>
> 1 Corinthians 3:9–10

C. The words of the New Testament are addressed to a body of people, not only to individuals. This includes the words about "building."

> In him you too are being built together to become a dwelling in which God lives by his Spirit.
>
> Ephesians 2:22, NIV

D. The Church (capital C for the worldwide group of people over the centuries and throughout the nations of the earth) is Jesus' idea. He is the Bridegroom and the Church is His Bride. He died to bring her to maturity so that she could be with Him forever.

As you therefore have received Christ Jesus the Lord, so walk in Him, rooted and built up in Him and established in the faith, as you have been taught, abounding in it with thanksgiving.

Colossians 2:6–7

II. Jesus Christ—the Solid Rock of Our Foundation

A. Jesus is the Rock, and we need to trust the Rock more than we trust what has been built on it.

No one can lay any foundation other than the one already laid, which is Jesus Christ.

1 Corinthians 3:11, NIV

1. Both the Old and New Testaments agree that Christ alone is our foundation.

This is what the Sovereign LORD says:

"See, I lay a stone in Zion,
a tested stone,
a precious cornerstone for a sure foundation;
the one who trusts will never be dismayed."

Isaiah 28:16, NIV

2. Peter quoted the Old Testament words from Isaiah 28:16 in one of his New Testament epistles:

In Scripture it says:

"See, I lay a stone in Zion,
a chosen and precious cornerstone,
and the one who trusts in him
will never be put to shame."

1 Peter 2:6, NIV

B. Jesus' own words confirm that He considers Himself our foundation. In Greek, the language of the New Testament, two different words are used for "rock." Jesus is a *petra,* a large, cliff-sized rock, and Peter, whose name comes from this word, is *petros,* a small stone. Jesus is the Rock of our salvation, the One upon whom the Church has been situated, and Peter is an apostle (a servant messenger) of the Lord in the foundation of the house. And all of us have "been built on the foundation of the apostles and prophets, Jesus Christ Himself being the chief cornerstone" (Ephesians 2:20).

He said to them, "But who do you say that I am?"

Simon Peter answered and said, "You are the Christ, the Son of the living God."

Jesus answered and said to him, "Blessed are you, Simon Bar-Jonah, for flesh and blood has not revealed this to you, but My Father who is in heaven. And I also say to you that you are Peter, and on this rock I will build My church, and the gates of Hades shall not prevail against it."

Matthew 16:15–18

1. As much as his name matches the word, Peter himself is not the Rock. "The LORD is my rock, my fortress and my deliverer; my God is my rock" (Psalm 18:2, NIV).

2. My soul waits in silence for God only . . . He only is my rock and my salvation, my stronghold; I shall not be greatly shaken. . . . My soul, wait silently for God alone, for my expectation is from Him. . . . In God is my salvation and my glory; the rock of my strength, and my refuge, is in God.

Psalm 62:1–2, 5, 7, NASB

3. Let it be known to you all, and to all the people of Israel, that by the name of Jesus Christ of Nazareth, whom you crucified, whom God raised from the dead, by Him this man stands here before you whole. This is the "stone which was rejected by you builders, which has become the chief cornerstone." Nor is there salvation in any other, for there is no other name under heaven given among men by which we must be saved.

Acts 4:10–12

4. He only is my rock and my salvation;

He is my defense;
I shall not be moved.

Psalm 62:6

C. The four stages of laying a proper foundation include the following:
1. Personal confrontation by Christ (see Matthew 16:16).
2. A direct, spiritual revelation of Christ (see John 16:13–14).
3. A personal acknowledgment of Christ (see John 17:3; 1 John 5:13, 20; 2 Timothy 1:12).
4. An open and personal confession of Christ (see Job 22:21; 2 Timothy 1:12).

III. Hearing and Doing the Words of Christ
A. Once it has been laid, we can build on the firm foundation by hearing and doing the words of Christ Jesus. This is the essence of the building process.

Everyone who hears these words of Mine and acts on them, may be compared to a wise man who built his house on the rock. And the rain fell, and the floods came, and the winds blew and slammed against that house; and yet it did not fall, for it had been founded on the rock.

Everyone who hears these words of Mine and does not act on them, will be like a foolish man who built his house on the sand. The rain fell, and the floods came, and the winds blew and slammed against that house; and it fell—and great was its fall.

Matthew 7:24–27, NASB

Brethren, I commend you to God and to the word of His grace, which is able to build you up and give you an inheritance among all those who are sanctified.

Acts 20:32

B. The Bible is the written Word; Christ is the Living Word.
   1. In the beginning was the Word, and the Word was with God, and the Word was God.

John 1:1

   2. The Word became flesh and dwelt among us, and we beheld His glory, the glory as of the only begotten of the Father, full of grace and truth.

John 1:14

   3. He was clothed with a robe dipped in blood, and His name is called The Word of God.

Revelation 19:13

C. Our relationship to the Bible must mirror our relationship to Christ Himself. The test of our discipleship is the keeping of His Word.

"A little while longer and the world will see Me no more, but you will see Me. Because I live, you will live also. At that day you will know that I am in My Father, and you in Me, and I in you. He who has My commandments and keeps them, it is he who loves Me. And he who loves Me will be loved by My Father, and I will love him and manifest Myself to him."

Judas (not Iscariot) said to Him, "Lord, how is it that You will manifest Yourself to us, and not to the world?"

Jesus answered and said to him, "If anyone loves Me, he will keep My word; and My Father will love him, and We will come to him and make Our home with him."

John 14:19–23

D. The test of our love for Christ and the release of God's favor toward us tie directly to our devotion to His Word.

He who says, "I know Him," and does not keep His commandments, is a liar, and the truth is not in him. But whoever keeps His word, truly the love of God is perfected in him. By this we know that we are in Him.

1 John 2:4–5

E. Jesus Christ manifests Himself to us, His disciples, through God's Word as it is heard, kept and obeyed.

1. It shall come to pass in the last days, says God,

> That I will pour out of My Spirit on all flesh;
> Your sons and your daughters shall prophesy,
> Your young men shall see visions,
> Your old men shall dream dreams.

Acts 2:17

2. May His light grow in us as we abide in His Word and are filled with His Spirit.

> Do not quench the Spirit. Do not despise prophecies. Test all things; hold fast what is good.

1 Thessalonians 5:19–21

F. God establishes His abiding presence with His disciples through His Word, which causes us to bear much fruit and avoid much error.

> Abide in Me, and I in you. As the branch cannot bear fruit of itself, unless it abides in the vine, neither can you, unless you abide in Me.

> I am the vine, you are the branches. He who abides in Me, and I in him, bears much fruit; for without Me you can do nothing. . . . If you abide in Me, and My words abide in you, you will ask what you desire, and it shall be done for you. By this My Father is glorified, that you bear much fruit; so you will be My disciples.

John 15:4–5, 7–8

1. In the beginning God created the heavens and the earth. The earth was without form, and void; and darkness was on the face of the deep. And the Spirit of God was hovering over the face of the waters. Then God said . . .

Genesis 1:1–3

2. By the word of the LORD the heavens were made,

> And all the host of them by the breath of His mouth.

Psalm 33:6

3. If anyone says to you, "Look, here is the Christ!" or "There!" do not believe it. For false christs and false prophets will rise and show great signs and wonders to deceive, if possible, even the elect. See, I have told you beforehand.

Matthew 24:23–25

4. The Spirit explicitly says that in later times some will fall away from the faith, paying attention to deceitful spirits and doctrines of demons, by means of the hypocrisy of liars seared in

their own conscience as with a branding iron, men who forbid marriage and advocate abstaining from foods which God has created to be gratefully shared in by those who believe and know the truth.

1 Timothy 4:1–3, NASB

5. Above all, you must understand that no prophecy of Scripture came about by the prophet's own interpretation. For prophecy never had its origin in the will of man, but men spoke from God as they were carried along by the Holy Spirit.

2 Peter 1:20–21, NIV

6. God's Word and God's Spirit united in our lives contain all the creative authority and power of God Himself. Through the combination of the written and Living Word, the Word and the Spirit, God will supply every need and will work out His perfect will, purpose and destiny for us. Built on the foundation of Jesus Christ, the Word Himself, we can expect to flourish—from now to eternity.

> The words of the LORD are pure words,
>   Like silver tried in a furnace of earth,
> Purified seven times.

Psalm 12:6

Reflection Questions

Lesson 1: The Foundation for All Believers

(Answers to these questions can be found in the back of the study guide.)

1. Fill in the blank:
   To be well-built, any structure requires a strong _____.
   To be a mature and successful believer, you must have a firm _____ of faith.

2. Referring back to section II. C., what are the four stages of laying a proper foundation in Christ?
   (1) _____
   (2) _____
   (3) _____
   (4) _____

3. Multiple choice: Choose the best answer from this list.
   (a) Jesus Christ
   (b) sound doctrine
   (c) the Church
   (d) good teaching
   The foundation of the Christian faith is _____.

4. Fill in the blank: "Jesus is the _____ of our salvation. The stone which the builders rejected has become the chief _____."

5. Whose responsibility is it to build on top of your faith foundation?
   (a) God's (b) Your pastor or more mature friends (c) Your own

Personal Application Question

6. Think about your own foundation in Christ. Is it sound? Immovable? Strong enough to build on? Glancing at the lesson titles in the table of contents, can you already spot an area where your foundational beliefs may be weaker than you would like? What area(s) need strengthening? How will you accomplish this?

LESSON 2

THE AMAZING WORD OF GOD

I. No Ordinary Book

A. The Bible, the Word of God, is no ordinary book. Composed by men who were inspired by God's Holy Spirit, the Scriptures embody His foundational plan for human beings on the earth. Without the Word of God, His salvation purpose and human destiny could not be handed down from one generation to another.

B. Through the Bible, God Himself speaks to every person, directly and personally. The words contained in the Word inform us, encourage us, cleanse us, sanctify us and make us partakers of the very nature of our Father God. They give us wisdom and power to overcome the powers of darkness, so that each one of us can live a victorious life in Christ Jesus.

C. Believers consider the Word of God to be authoritative. We base our faith-filled worldview on it. Our estimation of its authority is based partly on firsthand experience as well as vicarious experience. But—essentially proving its own authoritativeness—we look to the words of the Bible itself for proofs of the reliability of its source, purpose and benefits.

II. The Authority of the Word of God

A. The source of the Word of God. The Word of God is the very breath of God Himself. It originated in heaven. God "breathed" by His Spirit and men were inspired to write, becoming channels through whom His Word could be given to the rest of the human race. Here is what the written Word says about its own origin:

1. All Scripture is given by inspiration of God, and is profitable for doctrine, for reproof, for correction, for instruction in righteousness, that the man of God may be complete, thoroughly equipped for every good work.

   2 Timothy 3:16–17

2. No prophecy of Scripture is of any private interpretation, for prophecy never came by the will of man, but holy men of God spoke as they were moved by the Holy Spirit.

2 Peter 1:20–21

3. Thy word is true from the beginning.

Psalm 119:160, KJV

4. Forever, O LORD,

Your word is settled in heaven.

Psalm 119:89

5. In heaven, in God's being, the Word of God begins and becomes established and settled. When God "breathed" (often referred to as the wind of the essence of His Spirit, or *pneuma* in Greek) upon receptive people, the Word came into their minds and hearts. Thus breathed upon or moved upon, they began to speak about it. If scribes were present, they began to write it down.

The Son of God, Jesus, called the Scriptures the Word of God and declared that it "cannot be broken" (John 10:35).

B. What is the purpose of the Word of God? We have 66 individual books that, collected together into one volume, constitute what we know as the Bible. What is God's purpose for such an unusual book? His Word tells us:

1. All Scripture is given by inspiration of God, and is profitable for doctrine, for reproof, for correction, for instruction in righteousness, that the man of God may be complete, thoroughly equipped for every good work.

2 Timothy 3:16–17

2. As newborn babes, desire the sincere milk of the word, that ye may grow thereby.

1 Peter 2:2, KJV

3. "Man shall not live by bread alone, but by every word that proceeds from the mouth of God."

Matthew 4:4 (quoting Deuteronomy 8:3)

4. Though by this time you ought to be teachers, you need someone to teach you the elementary truths of God's word all over again. You need milk, not solid food! Anyone who lives on milk, being still an infant, is not acquainted with the teaching about righteousness. But solid food is for the mature, who by constant use have trained themselves to distinguish good from evil.

Hebrews 5:12–14, NIV

5. I have not departed from the commandment of His lips;

I have treasured the words of His mouth
More than my necessary food.

Job 23:12

6. Your words were found, and I ate them,

And Your word was to me the joy and rejoicing of my
heart;
For I am called by Your name,
O Lᴏʀᴅ God of hosts.

Jeremiah 15:16

C. What are the benefits of God's Word? As we take the Word of God into our spirits, the Holy Spirit releases life and light. As we read or listen to the written Word, we give ourselves to it and begin to love it. The Word lives inside. The living, breathing Word of God Himself (i.e., the Spirit of Jesus) quickens the written words so that they become revelatory. We will never get heavenly revelation without first having laid a foundation of the Word of God in our minds and spirits; the two go hand in hand.

By coming alive inside us, the Word helps us to keep pure and clean, free from sin, increasingly sanctified, able to overcome the devil.

The benefits of the Word of God multiply over time. No wonder God wants us to pay attention to His words. He wants His children to reflect His own image to the world, and to enjoy doing it.

1. How can a young man keep his way pure?

By living according to your word.

Psalm 119:9, ɴɪᴠ

2. Your word I have hidden in my heart,

That I might not sin against You.

Psalm 119:11

3. I write to you, young men,

because you are strong,
and the word of God lives in you,
and you have overcome the evil one.

1 John 2:14, ɴɪᴠ

4. Your word is a lamp to my feet

And a light to my path.

Psalm 119:105

5. The unfolding of Your words gives light;

It gives understanding to the simple.

Psalm 119:130, ɴᴀsʙ

6. My son, give attention to my words;

> Incline your ear to my sayings.
> Do not let them depart from your eyes;
> Keep them in the midst of your heart;
> For they are life to those who find them,
> And health to all their flesh.

Proverbs 4:20–22

7. You are already clean because of the word which I have spoken to you.

John 15:3

8. I pray for them. I do not pray for the world but for those whom You have given Me, for they are Yours. . . . Sanctify them by Your truth. Your word is truth.

John 17:9, 17

9. Brethren, I commend you to God and to the word of His grace, which is able to build you up and give you an inheritance among all those who are sanctified.

Acts 20:32

10. By his divine power, God has given us everything we need for living a godly life. We have received all of this by coming to know him, the one who called us to himself by means of his marvelous glory and excellence. And because of his glory and excellence, he has given us great and precious promises. These are the promises that enable you to share his divine nature and escape the world's corruption caused by human desires.

2 Peter 1:3–4, NLT

III. God's Word As a Source of Power

A. God's Word carries dividing power, like a "sword":

> The word of God is living and active. Sharper than any double-edged sword, it penetrates even to dividing soul and spirit, joints and marrow; it judges the thoughts and attitudes of the heart.

Hebrews 4:12, NIV

B. God's Word bears reflecting power, like a "mirror":

> Be doers of the Word [obey the message], and not merely listeners to it, betraying yourselves [into deception by reasoning contrary to the Truth]. For if anyone only listens to the Word without obeying it and being a doer of it, he is like a man who looks carefully at his [own] natural face in a mirror; for he thoughtfully observes himself, and then goes off and promptly forgets what he was like. But he who looks carefully into the faultless law, the [law] of liberty, and is faithful to it and perseveres in looking into it, being not a heedless listener who forgets but an

active doer [who obeys], he shall be blessed in his doing (his life of obedience).

James 1:22–25, AMP

C. God's Word conveys cleansing power, like a "detergent":

You are already clean because of the word which I have spoken to you.

John 15:3 (See also Ephesians 5:26.)

D. God's Word produces reproductive power, like a "seed":

. . . having been born again, not of corruptible seed but incorruptible, through the word of God.

1 Peter 1:23

E. God's Word imparts nourishing power, like "food":

Like newborn babies, long for the pure milk of the word, so that by it you may grow in respect to salvation.

1 Peter 2:2, NASB

Jesus answered, "It is written: 'Man does not live on bread alone, but on every word that comes from the mouth of God.'"

Matthew 4:4, NIV

You need milk, not solid food! Anyone who lives on milk, being still an infant, is not acquainted with the teaching about righteousness. But solid food is for the mature, who by constant use have trained themselves to distinguish good from evil.

Hebrews 5:12–14, NIV

F. God's Word serves as a guiding power, like a "lamp":

Thy word is a lamp unto my feet, and a light unto my path.

Psalm 119:105, KJV

We ourselves heard that voice from heaven when we were with him on the holy mountain. Because of that experience, we have even greater confidence in the message proclaimed by the prophets. You must pay close attention to what they wrote, for their words are like a lamp shining in a dark place—until the Day dawns, and Christ the Morning Star shines in your hearts.

2 Peter 1:18–19, NLT

G. God's Word is the power of the Gospel unto salvation:

I am not ashamed of the gospel of Christ: for it is the power of God unto salvation to every one that believeth.

Romans 1:16, KJV

IV. Receiving His Word
A. God's Word produces faith.

> Faith comes by hearing, and hearing by the word of God.
>
> Romans 10:17

B. God's Word brings peace.

> The peace of God, which transcends all understanding, will guard your hearts and your minds in Christ Jesus.
>
> Philippians 4:7, NIV

> [My word] will not return to me empty,
>   but will accomplish what I desire
>   and achieve the purpose for which I sent it.
> You will go out in joy
>   and be led forth in peace;
>   the mountains and hills
>   will burst into song before you,
>   and all the trees of the field
>   will clap their hands.
>
> Isaiah 55:11–12, NIV

C. God's Word cleanses our way.

> How can a young man cleanse his way?
> By taking heed according to Your word.
>
> Psalm 119:9

D. God's Word begins the process of change.

> The law of the LORD is perfect, converting the soul;
> The testimony of the LORD is sure, making wise the simple.
>
> Psalm 19:7

E. God's Word causes transformation.

> Do not be conformed to this world, but be transformed by the renewing of your mind, so that you may prove what the will of God is, that which is good and acceptable and perfect.
>
> Romans 12:2, NASB

F. God's Word works! It will not return to Him void. It will be productive in your life.

> So will My word be which goes forth from My mouth; it will not return to Me empty, without accomplishing what I desire, and without succeeding in the matter for which I sent it.
>
> Isaiah 55:11, NASB

V. How to Study Your Bible

A. Why should we study the Bible?

    1. We should study the Bible because Jesus said we should (see John 5:39). Those who searched the Scriptures daily were commended as being "noble" (see Acts 17:11).

2. We should study the Bible because Solomon (the wisest man of his day) wrote:

> My son, give attention to my words;
> Incline your ear to my sayings.
> Do not let them depart from your eyes;
> Keep them in the midst of your heart;
> For they are life to those who find them,
> And health to all their flesh.
>
> Proverbs 4:20–22

3. We should study the Bible because Peter taught that we are to desire the milk of the Word (see 1 Peter 2:2–4).

4. We should study the Bible because Jeremiah gave us the example of "eating" the Word as one eats bread for daily sustenance:

> Your words were found, and I ate them,
> And Your word was to me the joy and rejoicing of my
>   heart;
> For I am called by Your name,
> O Lord God of hosts.
>
> Jeremiah 15:16

5. We should study the Bible because James taught that studying the Word is like looking into a mirror of liberty, where we learn our rights in Christ:

> Be doers of the word, and not hearers only, deceiving yourselves. For if anyone is a hearer of the word and not a doer, he is like a man observing his natural face in a mirror; for he observes himself, goes away, and immediately forgets what kind of man he was. But he who looks into the perfect law of liberty and continues in it, and is not a forgetful hearer but a doer of the work, this one will be blessed in what he does.
>
> James 1:22–25

B. Practical suggestions for spiritual growth include the following:
   1. Read both the text and the context. (See Deuteronomy 17:19.) Glean basic ideas first and learn more about the background as you go. Start with the gospels (Matthew, Mark, Luke and John).
   2. Acknowledge what you read. (See 2 Corinthians 1:13.) You will learn to personalize the Word, seeing the words of the Bible as "now words" that convey God's thoughts for you.
   3. Read prayerfully with the Holy Spirit's help. Take note of whatever stands out to you. (See, for an example, Daniel 10:21.)
   4. Mark up your Bible. The cover of your Bible may read, "Holy Bible," but that does not mean you have to preserve the pages unmarked and unwrinkled. I recommend that you underline words and verses that carry special meaning for you, and that

you take notes in the margins. Before long, your favorite Bible will become an old friend, and you will glean even more from it because you have a history with it.

5. Study themes such as redemption and ask yourself questions. Ask "how," "when," "where" and "why" questions.

6. Study the life of a significant person in the Bible and ask yourself questions such as the following:

   a. Why did God choose this person?

   b. What did this person do (or not do) to comply with God's requirements?

   c. What process did God use to bring this person into the fullness of His purpose?

   d. What lessons can I learn from this person's life, especially as I learn faith and patience? (See Hebrews 6:12 and Romans 15:4.)

7. Use a good study Bible and concordance. As you study, cross-reference other materials. Take advantage of electronic search capabilities and other tools that you have available.

8. Use a *Strong's* or a *Young's Concordance* or another exhaustive version-based concordance. With these more complete resources, available in bound book format or online, research the original meaning and usage of specific words.

9. Use a lexicon. To supplement a complete concordance, use Greek and Hebrew lexicons to study word origins, other translation options, and other places that the word appears in Scripture.

10. Surround yourself with other believers. Become part of a group Bible study. Sit under skilled Bible teachers who can present both the historical and contextual understandings as well as the current-day applications of the Word for the present generation.

11. Grow in the Word of God. Look into the mirror of His Word and gaze upon His great beauty. As you do so, you will begin to reflect His likeness (see 2 Corinthians 3:18). You have a relationship with the living Word Himself, Jesus.

The Word became flesh and dwelt among us, and we beheld His glory, the glory as of the only begotten of the Father, full of grace and truth.

John 1:14

Reflection Questions

Lesson 2: The Amazing Word of God

(Answers to these questions can be found in the back of the study guide.)

1. In Psalm 119, nearly every verse mentions the Word of God directly or by a synonym: law, precept, ways, commandments, decrees, statutes, promise, ordinances—except only five verses. What are those five verses?

   _____

   _____

   _____

   _____

   _____

2. Fill in the blank: Studying the Word is like looking into a _____ of liberty, where we learn our rights in Christ.

3. What are three purposes of the Word of God?

   _____

   _____

   _____

4. What are three benefits of the Word of God?

   _____

   _____

   _____

5. The Word of God is more than ink on paper or words from heaven. The Word of God is what *person?* _____

Personal Application Question

6. Review section V. B., "practical suggestions for spiritual growth," and think about what you are currently doing to enhance your personal spiritual growth. Write down one thing you feel you are doing well and one new approach that you want to begin.

LESSON 3

GOD IN THREE PERSONS

I. The Three in One

  A. The triune nature of the Godhead is one of the most profound
     mysteries of Christianity. The three distinct persons of the God-
     head are the Father, the Son (Jesus Christ) and the Holy Spirit.
     Each person of the Godhead is fully God, none less than the
     other, while at the same time being *all together* fully God.

     How can God express unity and plurality at the same time?
     Human beings find themselves baffled and intrigued at the same
     time. Given our human limitations, we tend to elevate God in
     one of His persons more than others, showing relational prefer-
     ence for the Father or Jesus or the Spirit. Although maintaining
     balance proves difficult, our spiritual lives can stagnate without
     an awareness of God's "threeness."

  B. We must explore the two paradoxical concepts of unity and
     distinctness within the Trinity of the Godhead.

     1. Unity within the Godhead

        a. When God liberated the children of Israel from Egypt,
           He called them away from the polytheism (the worship of
           many gods) that they had learned there, instructing them
           that the God of Abraham, Isaac and Jacob is the only God
           (singular) in heaven: "Hear, O Israel: The LORD our God,
           the LORD is one!" (Deuteronomy 6:4).

        b. You shall have no other gods before Me. You shall not make
           for yourself a carved image—any likeness of anything that
           is in heaven above, or that is in the earth beneath, or that
           is in the water under the earth; you shall not bow down
           to them nor serve them. For I, the LORD your God, am a
           jealous God, visiting the iniquity of the fathers upon the
           children to the third and fourth generations of those who
           hate Me, but showing mercy to thousands, to those who
           love Me and keep My commandments.

You shall not take the name of the LORD your God in vain, for the LORD will not hold him guiltless who takes His name in vain.

Exodus 20:3–7

c. The one-God theme predominates throughout the Old and New Testaments. (See, for example, Isaiah 45:5; Jeremiah 10:1–6; John 17:3.)

"You are my witnesses, O Israel!" says the LORD.
  "You are my servant.
You have been chosen to know me, believe in me,
  and understand that I alone am God.
There is no other God—
  there never has been, and there never will be."

Isaiah 43:10, NLT

Therefore concerning the eating of things offered to idols, we know that an idol is nothing in the world, and that there is no other God but one.

1 Corinthians 8:4

2. Distinction of Persons within the Godhead
   a. The personhood of this One God has three distinctive expressions, and those three expressions did not begin with the birth of Jesus. Consider Genesis 1:26, which reads, "God said, 'Let Us make man in Our image, according to Our likeness.'" The use of the words "Us" and "Our" in this verse about the Creation refers to a plurality within the Godhead.
   b. Moving into the New Testament, we see that all three distinct expressions of God are portrayed at the baptism of Jesus:

When all the people were baptized, it came to pass that Jesus also was baptized; and while He prayed, the heaven was opened. And the Holy Spirit descended in bodily form like a dove upon Him, and a voice came from heaven which said, "You are My beloved Son; in You I am well pleased."

Luke 3:21–22

Here we see the Son being empowered by the Holy Spirit while the Father speaks His approval from heaven. As we move through the accounts of Jesus' life on earth, we see that Jesus the Son, who was sent by the Father (see 1 John 4:10) and who returned to the Father (see John 17:13), is now seated at His right hand in heaven (see Hebrews 1:3; 12:2). The Spirit, who was promised by the Father, was sent by the Son after His ascension to be with His people (see Matthew 28:19; John 14:16–23; Acts 2:33; 2 Corinthians 13:14).

c. These three Persons of the Trinity, Father, Son and Holy Spirit, are indeed Persons, not merely manifestations or modes of God Almighty. "Manifestations" cannot converse with one another. Neither do they express mutual affection for one another. These are expressions and actions of *persons* (see John 17).

d. At the same time, in His plurality, God is not divided. "In Him [Jesus] all the fullness of Deity dwells in bodily form" (Colossians 2:9, NASB). Jesus is no less God than the Father Himself (see John 1:1). Scripture also equates the Holy Spirit with God. When Peter rebuked Ananias for lying to the Holy Spirit, he said: "You have not lied to men but to God" (Acts 5:3–4).

e. This should not be too hard for us to comprehend, once we realize that we ourselves have been made in the image of God, and as human beings we are "triune" as well: (1) spirit, (2) soul (mind, emotions) and (3) body, one individual enriched because of the varied expressions of his or her personhood.

II. God As Father

A. He is a God who can be encountered.

1. "Who are You? What is Your name?" This question has been asked throughout the ages by all truth-seekers.

Moses said to God, "Indeed, when I come to the children of Israel and say to them, 'The God of your fathers has sent me to you,' and they say to me, 'What is His Name?' what shall I say to them?"

Exodus 3:13

2. God said to Moses, "I AM WHO I AM." And He said, "Thus you shall say to the children of Israel, 'I AM has sent me to you.'"

Exodus 3:14

In other words, He is the ever-present One, the God who is always in the present tense. He is not the God only of past history or the God of the future. In addition, the God who is always present is approachable. He is now. He is here. He wants a living, vibrant relationship with each person that He has made. He wants to be encountered. He wants His creatures to know Him.

B. Perhaps the greatest revelation of all is that God Almighty is our *Father*.

The apostle Paul wrote: "Grace to you and peace from God our Father and the Lord Jesus Christ" (Ephesians 1:2), and "For this reason I bow my knees to the Father of the Lord Jesus Christ, from whom the whole family in heaven and earth is named" (Ephesians 3:14–15).

God wants to gather His family. He desires fellowship. He wants us to address Him as "Father," even "Daddy" or "Abba," using terms of honor and endearment. Throughout both the Old and the New Testaments, His desire shines through.

C. This revelation of Fatherhood appears under both the Old Covenant and the New Covenant.

   1. Under the Old Covenant (from the Old Testament):
      a. Deuteronomy 32:6—"Is He not your Father?"
      b. Psalm 68:5—"A father of the fatherless . . ."
      c. Psalm 103:13—"As a father pities his children, so the LORD . . ."
      d. Isaiah 9:6—"His name will be called . . . Everlasting Father"
      e. Malachi 2:10—"Have we not all one Father?"

   2. Under the New Covenant (from the New Testament):
      a. Matthew 7:11—"how much more will your Father who is in heaven give good things to those who ask Him!"
      b. Matthew 23:9—" . . . for One is your Father . . ."
      c. Luke 11:2—"When you pray, say: Our Father in heaven. . . ."
      d. John 1:14—" . . . the only begotten of the Father, full of grace and truth."
      e. 1 Corinthians 8:6—"There is one God, the Father"
      f. Ephesians 4:6—" . . . one God and Father of all, who is above all, and through all, and in you all."
      g. Philippians 2:11—"Every tongue should confess that Jesus Christ is Lord, to the glory of God the Father."
      h. Hebrews 12:9—"Shall we not . . . be in subjection to the Father of spirits and live?"

III. Jesus As Messiah

A. Whereas Moses asked God, "Who are You?" Jesus turned the question around and asked His disciples, "Who do you say that I am?" (Matthew 16:15). He was probing to see what they were hearing from the people. Their answers varied:

   1. "John the Baptist" (who had been beheaded, which would have meant that he had come back from the dead). Perhaps Jesus' prophetic message was like John's. Perhaps the same crowds that had once followed John were now following Jesus. Perhaps it was the miracles, or maybe even the guilty conscience of the one replying (see Matthew 14:1–12).

   2. "Elijah the Prophet" (who, as prophesied in Malachi 4:5, would return before the "great and dreadful day of the LORD"). Perhaps the listeners remembered Malachi's words. Perhaps Jesus' type of prophetic ministry reminded them of Elijah's.

   3. " . . . Jeremiah the Prophet" (probably because of His compassionate ministry to the people; Jeremiah was known as the "weeping prophet").

B. "But who do *you* say that I am?" The rest of the disciples stayed silent, but Simon Peter spoke up:

"You are the Christ, the Son of the living God."

Jesus answered and said to him, "Blessed are you, Simon Bar-Jonah, for flesh and blood has not revealed this to you, but My Father who is in heaven."

Matthew 16:16–17

1. Ultimately, this is the question that every person throughout the ages must answer. Our reply to that single question, "Who do you say that I am?" will determine our present and our future destiny.

2. Jesus confronted Peter. Peter had not somehow come up with a creative idea about Jesus' identity. His natural senses did not help him know. He did not just happen to hit on the right choice. The Father revealed it to him through the Holy Spirit.

3. Jesus confronts each of us. The same spirit of revelation must show each of us who Jesus is. It takes God to know God.

C. Jesus the Messiah fulfills the New Covenant.

1. Behold, the days are coming, says the LORD, when I will make a new covenant with the house of Israel and with the house of Judah—not according to the covenant that I made with their fathers in the day that I took them by the hand to lead them out of the land of Egypt, My covenant which they broke, though I was a husband to them, says the LORD. But this is the covenant that I will make with the house of Israel after those days, says the LORD: I will put My law in their minds, and write it on their hearts; and I will be their God, and they shall be My people.

Jeremiah 31:31–33

2. Behold, the former things have come to pass,

And new things I declare;
Before they spring forth I tell you of them.

Isaiah 42:9

3. I will sprinkle clean water on you, and you shall be clean; I will cleanse you from all your filthiness and from all your idols. I will give you a new heart and put a new spirit within you; I will take the heart of stone out of your flesh and give you a heart of flesh. I will put My Spirit within you and cause you to walk in My statutes, and you will keep My judgments and do them.

Ezekiel 36:25–27

4. I will give them one heart, and I will put a new spirit within them, and take the stony heart out of their flesh, and give them

a heart of flesh, that they may walk in My statutes and keep My judgments and do them; and they shall be My people, and I will be their God.

Ezekiel 11:19–20

5. God was in Christ reconciling the world to Himself, not imputing their trespasses to them, and has committed to us the word of reconciliation.

Now then, we are ambassadors for Christ, as though God were pleading through us: we implore you on Christ's behalf, be reconciled to God. For He made Him who knew no sin to be sin for us, that we might become the righteousness of God in Him.

2 Corinthians 5:19–21

6. . . . and by Him to reconcile all things to Himself, by Him, whether things on earth or things in heaven, having made peace through the blood of His cross.

And you, who once were alienated and enemies in your mind by wicked works, yet now He has reconciled in the body of His flesh through death, to present you holy, and blameless, and above reproach in His sight.

Colossians 1:20–22

7. May the God of peace who brought up our Lord Jesus from the dead, that great Shepherd of the sheep, through the blood of the everlasting covenant, make you complete in every good work to do His will, working in you what is well pleasing in His sight, through Jesus Christ, to whom be glory forever and ever. Amen.

Hebrews 13:20–21

IV. The Person of the Holy Spirit

A. The Holy Spirit is the third Person of the Godhead.

1. From the words of Jesus:

a. When He, the Spirit of truth, has come, He will guide you into all truth; for He will not speak on His own authority, but whatever He hears He will speak; and He will tell you things to come. He will glorify Me, for He will take of what is Mine and declare it to you. All things that the Father has are Mine. Therefore I said that He will take of Mine and declare it to you.

John 16:13–15

b. You shall receive power when the Holy Spirit has come upon you; and you shall be witnesses to Me in Jerusalem, and in all Judea and Samaria, and to the end of the earth.

Acts 1:8

2. The most overlooked Person of the Godhead

    a. The Holy Spirit seems to be the most misunderstood and least appreciated member of the Trinity. Yet, He is the most vital in terms of personal conversion, growth in Christ, and ongoing building of God's glorious Kingdom on the earth.

    b. The Spirit may be the third Person of the Godhead, but that does not mean He is in a tertiary position or third-best. Part of this misunderstanding comes from the fact that His work is *never* to call attention to Himself, but only to exalt the Lord Jesus (see John 16:14).

B. The Holy Spirit is a Person. People find it too easy to think of Him as an "it." He is far more than an invisible influence, as some suggest. He is a real person, with His own mind, His own feelings, His own ability to communicate—just as the Father and the Son are real persons.

  1. Jesus explained how advantageous His imminent departure (death) would be, because He would then send His Holy Spirit to dwell intimately with Jesus' disciples, then and throughout the coming centuries (see John 16:7–15).

  2. He speaks (see Acts 8:29).

  3. He strives (see Genesis 6:3).

  4. He can be lied against (see Acts 5:3).

  5. He can be grieved (see Ephesians 4:30).

  6. He can be sinned against (see Mark 3:29).

  7. He searches all things (see 1 Corinthians 2:10–11).

  8. He makes intercession for us (see Romans 8:26).

  9. He distributes gifts (see 1 Corinthians 2:11).

 10. He is called the Counselor (see John 15:26).

 11. He is called the Comforter or Helper (see John 14:26).

C. Consider the deity of the Holy Spirit:

  1. He is specifically called "God" (see Acts 5:4; 2 Corinthians 3:17).

  2. He is eternal (see Hebrews 9:14).

  3. He is omnipresent (see Psalm 139:7).

  4. He is the Spirit of Life (see Romans 8:2).

  5. He is the Spirit of Truth (see John 16:13).

  6. He participated in the Creation (see Genesis 1:2).

  7. He participates in regeneration (see John 3:8).

  8. Jesus was raised from the dead by the Spirit (see Romans 8:11).

V. The Amazing Love of God

A. Behold, the love of God! This God who is Three-in-One *loves* the world He has created, and every individual person who has ever lived in it, including those yet to be born. "Behold what manner of love the Father has bestowed on us, that we should be called children of God!" (1 John 3:1).

B. God the Father proved His love by sending Jesus, His own Son, to live and die among us, so that He could send His Spirit, to underline His love emphatically: "God so loved the world that He gave His only begotten Son, that whoever believes in Him should not perish but have everlasting life" (John 3:16).

1. In this the love of God was manifested toward us, that God has sent His only begotten Son into the world, that we might live through Him.

1 John 4:9

2. He who did not spare His own Son, but delivered Him up for us all, how shall He not with Him also freely give us all things?

Romans 8:32

3. I am persuaded that neither death nor life, nor angels nor principalities nor powers, nor things present nor things to come, nor height nor depth, nor any other created thing, shall be able to separate us from the love of God which is in Christ Jesus our Lord.

Romans 8:38–39

C. This is the God we worship and love in return. He is the One we obey and serve with grateful hearts. "There are three that testify" (1 John 5:7, NIV)—the Father, His Son Jesus Christ and the Holy Spirit.

Reflection Questions

Lesson 3: God in Three Persons

(Answers to these questions can be found in the back of the study guide.)

1. Fill in the blank: The one God is a Triune Being, expressed as the
_____, the _____, and the _____ _____.

2. Multiple choice. Choose the best word from this list:
(a) manifestations
(b) persons
Our one God expresses Himself fully in three _____.

3. Multiple choice. Choose the best word from this list:
(a) polytheism
(b) slavery
When God liberated the children of Israel from Egypt, He called
them away from the _____ that they had
learned there.

4. True or false:
God first revealed Himself as triune when Jesus was born. _____
The Holy Spirit likes to call attention to Himself. _____
Jesus' death made it possible for His disciples to receive the Holy
Spirit. _____

5. Fill in the blank: The earliest plural mention of the one God in the
Bible is in the book of _____.

Personal Application Question

6. What does it mean to say, "It takes God to know God"? What has
been your personal experience in this regard?

LESSON 4

GOD'S PLAN FOR SALVATION

I. The Wages of Sin

    A. The theme verse for any discussion of salvation must be Romans 6:23: "The wages of sin is death, but the gift of God is eternal life in Christ Jesus our Lord." Sin costs something to us; we pay "wages" to it. And those wages are ultimate in nature—nothing less than death. The cost to each and every person is the same, and we will find no escape clause apart from the Son of God.

    B. Sin is our inward spiritual attitude of rebellion toward God, which is expressed in outward acts of disobedience. In other words, we want to be independent of God. We prefer to be self-directive. We may not commit what we think of as major sins, such as murder or adultery, but we can't help but commit lesser sins as we go through our days "doing our own thing."

        Isaiah put it this way: "All we like sheep have gone astray; we have turned, every one, to his own way; and the LORD has laid on Him the iniquity of us all" (Isaiah 53:6). Each human being ever born is a sinner, and our acts of disobedience cut us off from fellowship with God. Jesus Christ, the Son of God and Messiah, came to save us from our sins.

II. Sin

    A. We were created to give God pleasure. When we worship Him, we participate in heavenly praise and we ourselves taste His pleasure.

> Thou art worthy, O Lord, to receive glory and honour and power: for thou hast created all things, and for thy pleasure they are and were created.
>
> Revelation 4:11, KJV

> You will show me the path of life; in your presence is fullness of joy; at Your right hand are pleasures forevermore.
>
> Psalm 16:11

    B. All have sinned. We humans fall far, far short of our Creator's original goal for us.

1. All have sinned, and come short of the glory of God (Romans 3:23, KJV).

2. Even though they knew God, they did not honor Him as God or give thanks (Romans 1:21, NASB).

3. They became futile in their speculations, and their foolish heart was darkened. Professing to be wise, they became fools (Romans 1:21–22, NASB).

4. The human heart is the most deceitful of all things, and desperately wicked. Who really knows how bad it is? (Jeremiah 17:9, NLT).

C. Evil proceeds from the heart. When Jesus was asked about it, He listed at least thirteen evils that issue from the human heart: (1) evil thoughts, (2) adulteries, (3) fornications, (4) murders, (5) thefts, (6) covetousness, (7) wickedness, (8) deceit, (9) lasciviousness, (10) the "evil eye" (envy), (11) blasphemy (slander), (12) pride and (13) foolishness. These have been taken from Mark 7:21–22 (KJV).

D. Sin carries ultimate consequences.

1. Death becomes the ultimate result of sin. "When desire has conceived, it gives birth to sin; and sin, when it is full-grown, brings forth death" (James 1:15; see also Romans 5:12; 6:23).

2. The lake of fire is the final end of all unrepentant sinners (see Matthew 25:41).

> I saw the dead, small and great, standing before God, and books were opened. And another book was opened, which is the Book of Life. And the dead were judged according to their works, by the things which were written in the books. The sea gave up the dead who were in it, and Death and Hades delivered up the dead who were in them. And they were judged, each one according to his works. Then Death and Hades were cast into the lake of fire. This is the second death. And anyone not found written in the Book of Life was cast into the lake of fire.
>
> Revelation 20:12–15

3. The Spirit spoke to John when he was on the island called Patmos and listed some of the sinful states that led to this quite literal lake of fire:

> The fearful, and unbelieving, and the abominable, and murderers, and whoremongers, and sorcerers, and idolaters, and all liars, shall have their part in the lake which burneth with fire and brimstone: which is the second death.
>
> Revelation 21:8, KJV

III. The Purpose of the Death and Resurrection of Jesus Christ

A. Take a look at the life of Jesus Christ.

1. Jesus Himself never committed any sin. He never even thought a sinful thought. "We do not have a High Priest who cannot

sympathize with our weaknesses, but was in all points tempted as we are, yet without sin" (Hebrews 4:15; see also 1 Peter 2:22).

2. His whole purpose in coming to earth as a man was "to save sinners" (1 Timothy 1:15).

3. He received sinners—men, women and children—to Himself. "For I did not come to call the righteous, but sinners, to repentance" (Matthew 9:13; see also Luke 15:2).

B. Remember the cross of Jesus Christ.

1. The God-Man Jesus "Himself bore our sins in His body on the cross, so that we might die to sin and live to righteousness" (1 Peter 2:24, NASB).

2. Jesus died on the cross to bring sinful humankind to God: Christ suffered for our sins once for all time. He never sinned, but he died for sinners to bring you safely home to God. He suffered physical death, but he was raised to life in the Spirit.

1 Peter 3:18, NLT

C. Recall the Good News of Jesus Christ.

1. The Gospel message, preached by Jesus' disciples ever since His resurrection, is that (a) Jesus died for our sins, (b) was buried in the grave and (c) rose to life again after three days. Apostle-teacher Paul wrote:

I passed on to you what was most important and what had also been passed on to me. Christ died for our sins, just as the Scriptures said. He was buried, and he was raised from the dead on the third day, just as the Scriptures said.

1 Corinthians 15:3–4, NLT

2. Now that Jesus Christ is alive forevermore, having won out over death and the grave, people can be confident that He is able to bring them along with Him (see Hebrews 7:25).

3. Salvation, repentance and remission of sins would now be offered through the name of Jesus to all men and women everywhere and for all time (see Luke 24:47; Acts 4:12).

IV. How to Receive Salvation

A. People cannot save themselves. Salvation comes through personal faith in Jesus Christ alone, not through good works or any set of religious actions. We must turn from our sins and repent, believing that Jesus died and rose again for our sakes. Having received the risen Christ by faith into our hearts, we must publicly confess Him as Lord and Savior. Salvation happens by grace, through faith in the completed work of the cross of Jesus Christ.

As many as received Him, to them He gave the right to become children of God, to those who believe in His name: who were born, not of blood, nor of the will of the flesh, nor of the will of man, but of God.

John 1:12–13

B. The blood of Jesus Christ is all-powerful.

1. If we desire God's mercy, we must confess and forsake our sins. "People who conceal their sins will not prosper, but if they confess and turn from them, they will receive mercy" (Proverbs 28:13, NLT).

2. "If we confess our sins, He is faithful and just to forgive us our sins and to cleanse us from all unrighteousness" (1 John 1:9).

3. "The blood of Jesus Christ His Son cleanses (removes) us from all sin and guilt [keeps us cleansed from sin in all its forms and manifestations]" (1 John 1:7, AMP).

C. What are the steps to salvation?

1. To be saved, we must believe in our hearts that God has raised Jesus from the dead and confess with our mouth that Jesus Christ is Lord. The word *confess* means to agree with and to speak aloud.

If you confess with your mouth the Lord Jesus and believe in your heart that God has raised Him from the dead, you will be saved. For with the heart one believes unto righteousness, and with the mouth confession is made unto salvation.

Romans 10:9–10

2. If we come to Christ Jesus, He will not reject us:

All whom My Father gives (entrusts) to Me will come to Me; and the one who comes to Me I will most certainly not cast out [I will never, no never, reject one of them who comes to Me].

John 6:37, AMP

3. If we open the door of our heart, Jesus will come in:

Here I am! I stand at the door and knock. If anyone hears my voice and opens the door, I will come in and eat with him, and he with me.

Revelation 3:20, NIV

4. Receiving Christ gives us the power to become "sons of God." Now we know that we are born again.

As many as received Him, to them He gave the right to become children of God, to those who believe in His name: who were born, not of blood, nor of the will of the flesh, nor of the will of man, but of God.

John 1:12–13

D. Jesus' death and resurrection have gained us eternal life.

1. The Father grants eternal life to those who receive His Son Jesus. "The gift of God is eternal life in Christ Jesus our Lord" (Romans 6:23).

2. God testifies that we have eternal life through Jesus Christ: "This is what God has testified: He has given us eternal life, and this life is in his Son" (1 John 5:11, NLT).

3. We know we have eternal life.

> He who has the Son has life; he who does not have the Son of God does not have life. These things I have written to you who believe in the name of the Son of God, that you may know that you have eternal life, and that you may continue to believe in the name of the Son of God.
>
> 1 John 5:12–13

V. Salvation Gives Power to Overcome

A. Jesus Christ lives in our hearts by faith.

1. His Spirit takes up residence in our hearts. (See Galatians 2:20 and Ephesians 1:17.)

> I will ask the Father, and He will give you another Comforter (Counselor, Helper, Intercessor, Advocate, Strengthener, and Standby), that He may remain with you forever—the Spirit of Truth, Whom the world cannot receive (welcome, take to its heart), because it does not see Him or know and recognize Him. But you know and recognize Him, for He lives with you [constantly] and will be in you.
>
> John 14:16–17, AMP

2. As a result, we can say, "I can do all things through Christ who strengthens me" (Philippians 4:13).

3. As we continue to confess Christ before other people, He in turn will declare our names before His Father, standing in for our insufficiencies with His spotless righteousness (see Matthew 10:32).

4. Conversely, since we possess free will, we are capable of denying Him, too. Nobody will force us to continue to confess Him as Lord, any more than we were forced to surrender to His Lordship in the first place. And any of us who denies Christ before other people will in turn be denied by Him before His Father (see Matthew 10:33).

B. What does it mean to "overcome the world"?

1. Being born again guarantees that a person has the capacity to become an overcomer:

> Whatever is born of God overcomes the world. And this is the victory that has overcome the world—our faith. Who is he who overcomes the world, but he who believes that Jesus is the Son of God?
>
> 1 John 5:4–5

2. The Son of God gives us the power to overcome the world and its temptations—although often that will entail a fight. We can overcome all the temptations in the world because greater is He that is in us than he who is in the world (see 1 John 4:4).

3. We overcome the devil by the blood of the Lamb (Jesus) and testifying what that blood has done for us (see Revelation 12:11).

Reflection Questions

Lesson 4: God's Plan for Salvation

(Answers to these questions can be found in the back of the study guide.)

1. Multiple choice: Choose the best word from this list.
   (a) love
   (b) death
   (c) blood
   (d) fellowship
   The _____ of Jesus Christ is God's remedy to cleanse our hearts from all sin.

2. Fill in the blanks (two words): "This is a faithful saying and worthy of all acceptance, that Christ Jesus came into the world to _____ _____" (1 Timothy 1:15).

3. True or false:
   We were created to give God pleasure. ____
   Some sinners are worse than others. _____
   To be saved, we must say the "sinner's prayer," using certain words. _____

4. Romans 6:23 reads, "The wages of sin is death." What does this mean? Choose the right answer:
   (a) The situation is hopeless, because every person is going to die.
   (b) People owe something because of sin; they must pay for it by means of death.
   (c) Sin pays for itself—with death.

5. Fill in the blanks (two words): "Whatever is born of God overcomes the world. And this is the victory that has overcome the world— _____ _____" (1 John 5:4).

Personal Application Question

6. Write an account of your own salvation story, inserting at least two pertinent Scriptures.

LESSON 5

REPENTANCE FROM DEAD WORKS

I. A Fresh Start

A. Repentance is the foundation of faith. Before we can exercise faith, we must repent of our old ways of operating. Repentance prepares the way so that our hearts can respond in faith. God says, "Repent and believe," not "believe and repent."

B. No one is exempt from the need to repent—nor should anyone want to be exempt. "God overlooked people's ignorance about these things in earlier times, but now he commands everyone everywhere to repent of their sins and turn to him" (Acts 17:30, NLT). Repentance is the pathway to God.

II. Foundational for the Christian's Life

A. What is repentance? True repentance is an inward decision resulting in a change of mind. The word most commonly translated in the Old Testament as "to repent" meant literally, "to turn," "to return," or "to turn back," in an outward expression of action. By the time the New Testament was written, the meaning of the word had been expanded to emphasize the inward nature of true repentance.

   1. Primary Old Testament root word: *shubh.* It means to turn 180 degrees, to return, to go back, including turning from sin to God.

   2. Primary New Testament words: *metanoia* (noun form) and *metanoeo* (verb form), which apply less to a physical turning process and more to a change of mind. Sometimes the word used is the verb *epistrepho,* which means "turning," "return," or "turn about," more in the Old Testament sense. See some sample Scriptures below.

B. Review the primary Scriptures.

   1. Let us stop going over the basic teachings about Christ again and again. Let us go on instead and become mature in our understanding. Surely we don't need to start again with the

fundamental importance of repenting from evil deeds and placing our faith in God.

Hebrews 6:1, NLT

2. John came baptizing in the wilderness and preaching a baptism of repentance [*metanoia*] for the remission of sins.

Mark 1:4

3. After John was put in prison, Jesus came to Galilee, preaching the gospel of the kingdom of God, and saying, "The time is fulfilled, and the kingdom of God is at hand. Repent [*metanoeo*], and believe in the gospel."

Mark 1:14–15

4. He will be great in the sight of the Lord, and shall drink neither wine nor strong drink. He will also be filled with the Holy Spirit, even from his mother's womb. And he will turn [*epistrepho*] many of the children of Israel to the Lord their God.

Luke 1:15–16

5. Thus it is written, and thus it was necessary for the Christ to suffer and to rise from the dead the third day, and that repentance [*metanoia*] and remission of sins should be preached in His name to all nations, beginning at Jerusalem.

Luke 24:46–47

6. Peter said to them, "Repent [*metanoeo*], and let every one of you be baptized in the name of Jesus Christ for the remission of sins; and you shall receive the gift of the Holy Spirit."

Acts 2:38

III. Turning from Self to God
A. Renunciation of self-confidence allows us to turn toward God-confidence.
1. Our own way leads us astray. "All we like sheep have gone astray; we have turned, every one, to his own way" (Isaiah 53:6).
2. We must confess our sin, turn from sin and place our confidence in God. "'We have sinned. Punish us as you see fit, only rescue us today from our enemies.' Then the Israelites put aside their foreign gods and served the LORD" (Judges 10:15–16, NLT).
3. We must repent and turn toward God.

I did not prove disobedient to the heavenly vision, but kept declaring both to those of Damascus first, and also at Jerusalem and then throughout all the region of Judea, and even to the Gentiles, that they should repent and turn to God, performing deeds appropriate to repentance.

Acts 26:19–20, NASB

4. We must turn from our "idols" and serve God. (See 1 Thessalonians 1:8–9.) In our Western culture, our idolatry does not consist of worshiping little statues as much as ideologies and pursuits, such as humanism, entertainment, sports, education, patriotism or politics. Even religion itself. We have all kinds of idols or "small g" gods. Each idol has its own requirements and rules.

B. Why is "repentance" so important?

1. Repentance from dead works is essential for salvation (see Mark 1:15).

2. Repentance from dead works is commanded by God (see Acts 17:30).

3. Repentance from dead works is an outright gift from God (see Acts 11:18; 2 Timothy 2:25).

4. Repentance from dead works is a primary reason for Jesus' coming (see Luke 5:32).

5. Repentance from dead works is necessary to avoid destruction (see Luke 13:3, 5).

6. Repentance from dead works is part of the Lord's commission to His people (see Luke 24:47).

7. Repentance from dead works is desired by God for all humankind (see 2 Peter 3:9).

IV. Dead Works Defined

A. We have all gone our own way.

1. Sin means we are going our own way, operating by our own strength and initiative. (See Isaiah 53:6.)

2. Death results from sin. (Refer back to lesson 4.) "The wages of sin is death" (Romans 6:23).

3. Even our righteous acts are mere "filthy rags" before God.

> We are all like an unclean thing,
> And all our righteousnesses are like filthy rags;
> We all fade as a leaf,
> And our iniquities, like the wind,
> Have taken us away.
>
> Isaiah 64:6

B. Good works are never enough.

1. We cultivate good works in our effort to gain favor and earn grace in the eyes of God. However, "By grace you have been saved through faith, and that not of yourselves; it is the gift of God, not of works, lest anyone should boast" (Ephesians 2:8–9).

2. We will never be able to obtain God's mercy by the works of our hands.

When God our Savior revealed his kindness and love, he saved us, not because of the righteous things we had done, but because of his mercy. He washed away our sins, giving us a new birth and new life through the Holy Spirit.

Titus 3:4–5, NLT

God saved us and called us to live a holy life. He did this, not because we deserved it, but because that was his plan from before the beginning of time—to show us his grace through Christ Jesus.

2 Timothy 1:9, NLT

C. Religious works apart from faith are never enough.

   1. Although the Pharisees were very religious, their religiosity could not save them. Their religious works, undertaken by human strength and not by the faith-provided strength of God, rendered the worship a vain exercise (see Mark 7:7–9).

   2. The Pharisees' strenuous human efforts caused them to keep sinning—religiously. They accused Jesus and His disciples of not washing their hands often enough, while meantime they were breaking the fourth commandment (see Matthew 15:1–9). They just could not accept the fact that they were sinners.

D. "Works" are not all bad. What are some fruitful works?

   1. True "good works" manifest the genuineness of a disciple of Jesus. The Scriptures do encourage us to live fruitful lives.

Since the day we heard about you, we have not stopped praying for you and asking God to fill you with the knowledge of his will through all spiritual wisdom and understanding. And we pray this in order that you may live a life worthy of the Lord and may please him in every way: bearing fruit in every good work, growing in the knowledge of God.

Colossians 1:9–10, NIV

   2. The works of disciples should be inspired by the Holy Spirit rather than by human effort. "We are His workmanship, created in Christ Jesus for good works, which God prepared beforehand that we should walk in them" (Ephesians 2:10).

   3. The Father "prunes" us to eliminate barrenness and to ensure greater fruitfulness in the future.

I am the true vine, and My Father is the vinedresser. Every branch in Me that does not bear fruit He takes away; and every branch that bears fruit He prunes, that it may bear more fruit. You are already clean because of the word which I have spoken to you. Abide in Me, and I in you. As the branch cannot bear fruit of itself, unless it abides in the vine, neither can you, unless you abide in Me.

I am the vine, you are the branches. He who abides in Me, and I in him, bears much fruit; for without Me you can do nothing. If anyone does not abide in Me, he is cast out as a branch and is withered; and they gather them and throw them into the fire, and they are burned. If you abide in Me, and My words abide in you, you will ask what you desire, and it shall be done for you. By this My Father is glorified, that you bear much fruit; so you will be My disciples.

John 15:1–8

4. As our works correspond to our actions, we continue to demonstrate that we have genuine faith. (See James 2:20–26.)

V. Characteristics of Repentance

A. What are the components of repentance? God's Spirit dwelling within our hearts makes it possible for us to fulfill the requirements of true, godly repentance, which are as follows:

1. Godly sorrow (see 2 Corinthians 7:9–10)—The godly sorrow of David (see Psalm 32:3–5) and Peter (see Luke 22:62) brought true repentance, but the human sorrow of Esau (see Hebrews 12:17) and Judas (see Matthew 27:3–5) did not.

2. Self-examination—By daring to examine ourselves, we expose our sinfulness to the light. (See Psalm 139:23–24; Jeremiah 17:9; Lamentations 3:40.)

3. Confession to God—First of all, we talk to God about our sins, because "if we confess our sins, He is faithful and just to forgive us our sins and to cleanse us from all unrighteousness" (1 John 1:9; see also Proverbs 28:13).

4. Public confession—Do not underestimate the importance of public confession:

If you confess with your mouth Jesus as Lord, and believe in your heart that God raised Him from the dead, you will be saved; for with the heart a person believes, resulting in righteousness, and with the mouth he confesses, resulting in salvation.

Romans 10:9–10, NASB (see also Acts 19:18)

Public confession opens the way for healing (see James 5:16) and for the gift of the Holy Spirit (see Acts 2:38).

5. Forsaking of sin—Rejecting sin can seem costly at first, yet it always results in boundless blessings (see Acts 19:19; Proverbs 28:13; 2 Corinthians 5:15).

6. Reconciliation—God expects us to make the effort to be reconciled with those who have something against us (see Matthew 5:23–24).

7. Restitution—Restitution is endorsed in both the Old Testament (see Ezekiel 33:14–15) and the New Testament (see Luke 19:8–9, the story of Zacchaeus).

8. Good works—As the apostle Paul declared to King Agrippa:

I was not disobedient to the heavenly vision, but declared first to those in Damascus and in Jerusalem, and throughout all the region of Judea, and then to the Gentiles, that they should repent, turn to God, and do works befitting repentance.

Acts 26:19–20 (see also Luke 3:7–14; Daniel 4:27)

B. Repentance is a gift from God. In the story of the rich young ruler (see Mark 10:17–31), the disciples realized that the requirements to enter God's Kingdom far exceeded human strength. They asked, "Who then can be saved?" (Mark 10:26, NIV). And Jesus replied, "With man this is impossible, but not with God; all things are possible with God" (Mark 10:27, NIV). The Holy Spirit moves in our hearts to enable us to respond to the Gospel of the Kingdom with total commitment.

1. The God of our fathers raised up Jesus, whom you had put to death by hanging Him on a cross.

   He is the one whom God exalted to His right hand as a Prince and a Savior, to grant repentance to Israel, and forgiveness of sins.

   Acts 5:30–31, NASB

2. "If God gave them the same gift as he gave us, who believed in the Lord Jesus Christ, who was I to think that I could oppose God?"

   When they heard this, they had no further objections and praised God, saying, "So then, God has granted even the Gentiles repentance unto life."

   Acts 11:17–18, NIV

3. I tell you the truth. It is to your advantage that I go away; for if I do not go away, the Helper will not come to you; but if I depart, I will send Him to you. And when He has come, He will convict the world of sin, and of righteousness, and of judgment: of sin, because they do not believe in Me; of righteousness, because I go to My Father and you see Me no more; of judgment, because the ruler of this world is judged.

   John 16:7–11

4. They may come to their senses and escape from the snare of the devil, having been held captive by him to do his will.

   2 Timothy 2:26, NASB

5. The grace of God that brings salvation has appeared to all men, teaching us that, denying ungodliness and worldly lusts, we should live soberly, righteously, and godly in the present age, looking for the blessed hope and glorious appearing of our great God and Savior Jesus Christ, who gave Himself for us, that He might redeem us from every lawless deed and purify for Himself His own special people, zealous for good works.

   Titus 2:11–14

Reflection Questions

Lesson 5: Repentance from Dead Works

(Answers to these questions can be found in the back of the study guide.)

1. Fill in the blanks:

   Repentance is the _____ of faith.

   Repentance from dead works is an outright _____ from God.

   True repentance is an inward decision resulting in a _____ of mind.

2. True or false:

   The goal of the Christian life is to be a good person. _____

   Repentance is saying that you're sorry for what you have done. _____

   You cannot repent apart from God's help. _____

3. Multiple choice. Fill in the blanks with the best word from this list:

   (a) faith

   (b) love

   (c) works

   (d) repentance

   The first step in building a firm foundation is _____.

   James 2:20–26 tells us that we demonstrate that we have genuine faith by our _____.

4. What are the eight components of godly repentance? (See section V. A.) _____, _____, _____, _____, _____, _____, _____, _____

5. "We are His workmanship, created in Christ Jesus for good _____, which God prepared beforehand that we should walk in them" (Ephesians 2:10).

Personal Application Question

6. People often say, "I am a good person, so I believe I will go to heaven." Do you agree with this statement? Why or why not? Support your reasons with at least two Scripture passages.

LESSON 6

GRACE DEFINED

I. Fundamentals

  A. We begin and end in grace. The word *grace* is used one hundred and fifty times in the New Testament, primarily in the epistles. It is used as a salutation ("Grace and peace be with you"). And it is used as a closing ("The grace of God be with you"). This indicates to us that we too should begin and end everything with God's grace.

  B. As many as received Him, to them He gave the right to become children of God, even to those who believe in His name, who were born, not of blood nor of the will of the flesh nor of the will of man, but of God.

> And the Word became flesh, and dwelt among us, and we saw His glory, glory as of the only begotten from the Father, *full of grace and truth*. . . .
>
> For of His fullness we have all received, and grace upon grace. For the Law was given through Moses; grace and truth were realized through Jesus Christ.
>
> John 1:12–14, 16–17, NASB, emphasis added

  C. In the New Testament, two similar Greek words get translated into the English word *grace*. *Charis* means grace in general terms, while *charisma* is grace in the specific or grace made manifest, as a gift. When we use the plural of *charisma*, the word becomes *charismata*, which is where the English designation "charismatics" derives from.

  D. The Old Testament Hebrew terms *chen* and *ratsown* connote pleasantness, attractiveness and favor. Thus, "Noah found grace [*chen*, favor] in the eyes of the LORD" (Genesis 6:8). Thus, the word *grace* incorporates a sense of attractiveness or beauty. If we say someone is "graceful," we usually mean that person moves and behaves with poise and loveliness. The link between the Hebrew and biblical Greek meanings is easy to see, because anyone who manifests the grace of God is attractive to others.

E. Having found favor first with God, a grace-filled person finds favor in the sight of others as well. If you have truth without grace, you will not attract anyone to your message. Religion can be full of truth, but if it lacks grace, it becomes sour and unpalatable.

F. The writers of the epistles who bless their listeners and readers by starting and ending with greetings of grace and peace found their precedent in the Old Testament greeting:

> The LORD bless you and keep you; the LORD make His face shine upon you, and be gracious to you; the LORD lift up His countenance upon you, and give you peace.
>
> Numbers 6:24–26

This grace and peace comes from the countenance, or face, of the Lord God. When you are in His face (in His presence), you receive His grace and His peace. Peace cannot come without grace.

II. Grace versus Works

A. "Works" are what people do to try to obtain God's favor and righteous standing apart from Christ. Works do not work.

> By grace you have been saved through faith, and that not of yourselves; it is the gift of God, not of works, lest anyone should boast.
>
> Ephesians 2:8–9

B. Anything that you earn is, by definition, *not* grace. Grace is free. It cannot be earned. Religious people have the most trouble with this dynamic.

> There has also come to be at the present time a remnant according to God's gracious choice. But if it is by grace, it is no longer on the basis of works, otherwise grace is no longer grace.
>
> Romans 11:5–6, NASB

C. Our just God is also our Savior. Justice will usually lead to punishment. If we all got justice in terms of salvation, all of us would be doomed to hell. In His merciful graciousness, God has saved us from His own justice.

D. God's laws are immutable. But Jesus Christ, only Son of the Father God, is the end of the law. He has fulfilled the requirements. "Christ is the end of the law for righteousness to everyone who believes" (Romans 10:4).

III. Three Requirements for Receiving Grace

A. Humble yourself. "God resists the proud, but gives grace to the humble" (1 Peter 5:5, quoting Proverbs 3:34; see also James 4:6–7). When you humble yourself, you admit that you cannot make it without Him. Humbling yourself is a form of repentance. Grace is the remedy for sin, not the covering for it, and repentance is the vessel out of which we must drink grace.

B. Stop working and believe. Since each person apart from Christ receives his or her just reward, which is death (see Romans 6:23), we need to stop working for those wages and instead receive the rewards of grace. In order to do so, we will need to operate by a different kind of economy:

> Abraham was, humanly speaking, the founder of our Jewish nation. What did he discover about being made right with God? If his good deeds had made him acceptable to God, he would have had something to boast about. But that was not God's way. For the Scriptures tell us, "Abraham believed God, and God counted him as righteous because of his faith."
>
> When people work, their wages are not a gift, but something they have earned. But people are counted as righteous, not because of their work, but because of their faith in God who forgives sinners.
>
> Romans 4:1–5, NLT

C. Receive more of Christ. All grace is in Jesus Christ. To the degree that you embrace and receive Christ, you receive grace. (See again John 1:12, 17.) Daily, we must humble ourselves, determine to rely on Him and receive His grace. We do not need to pray the sinner's prayer multiple times, but we do need to receive grace— many, many times. It becomes a lifestyle.

IV. Benefits of Grace

A. Grace covers us with a protective shield:

> It is You who blesses the righteous man, O Lord,
> You surround him with *favor* as with a shield.
>
> Psalm 5:12, NASB, emphasis added

> The Lord God is a sun and shield; the Lord gives *grace*
>   and glory; no good thing does He withhold from
>   those who walk uprightly.
>
> Psalm 84:11, NASB, emphasis added

B. Grace (and favor) can be compared with a cloud filled with spring (or "latter") rain: "In the light of a king's face is life, and his favor is like a cloud with the spring rain" (Proverbs 16:15, NASB).

C. Grace is our tutor.

> The grace of God has appeared, bringing salvation to all men, instructing us to deny ungodliness and worldly desires and to live sensibly, righteously and godly in the present age, looking for the blessed hope and the appearing of the glory of our great God and Savior, Christ Jesus, who gave Himself for us to redeem us from every lawless deed, and to purify for Himself a people for His own possession, zealous for good deeds.
>
> Titus 2:11–14, NASB

D. His grace is enough. It covers every weakness. God told Paul:

> He [God] has said to me, "My grace is sufficient for you, for power is perfected in weakness." Most gladly, therefore, I will rather boast about my weaknesses, so that the power of Christ may dwell in me.
>
> 2 Corinthians 12:9, NASB

V. Apostle Paul's Secret

A. You cannot earn grace. The apostle Paul knew he could never have earned it and that nobody else could earn it, either. The gift of God's grace was the key to the apostle Paul's success. Paul did not refuse the gift when it was offered:

> I became a minister [of the gospel] according to the gift of the grace of God given to me by the effective working of His power.
>
> To me, who am less than the least of all the saints, this grace was given, that I should preach among the Gentiles the unsearchable riches of Christ.
>
> Ephesians 3:6–8

B. Great fruitfulness resulted from Paul's life as he ministered in and through the gift of the grace of God.

> By the grace of God I am what I am, and His grace toward me did not prove vain; but I labored even more than all of them, yet not I, but the grace of God with me.
>
> 1 Corinthians 15:10, NASB

VI. What Can You Do with Grace?

A. Speak grace.

> Let no unwholesome word proceed from your mouth, but only such a word as is good for edification according to the need of the moment, so that it will give grace to those who hear.
>
> Do not grieve the Holy Spirit of God, by whom you were sealed for the day of redemption. Let all bitterness and wrath and anger and clamor and slander be put away from you, along with all malice. Be kind to one another, tender-hearted, forgiving each other, just as God in Christ also has forgiven you.
>
> Ephesians 4:29–32, NASB

B. Pray for grace.

> I will pour out a spirit of grace and prayer on the family of David and on the people of Jerusalem. They will look on me whom they have pierced and mourn for him as for an only son. They will grieve bitterly for him as for a firstborn son who has died.
>
> Zechariah 12:10, NLT

C. Shout grace!

> This is the word of the LORD to Zerubbabel:
> "Not by might nor by power, but by My Spirit,"

Says the Lord of hosts.
"Who are you, O great mountain?
Before Zerubbabel you shall become a plain!
And he shall bring forth the capstone
With shouts of 'Grace, grace to it!'"

Zechariah 4:6–7

VII. Receive Grace

A. Come boldly. Step forward boldly and receive the full measure of grace that has been assigned to you by Jesus Himself.

> Since we have a great high priest who has passed through the heavens, Jesus the Son of God, let us hold fast our confession. For we do not have a high priest who cannot sympathize with our weaknesses, but One who has been tempted in all things as we are, yet without sin.
>
> Therefore let us draw near with confidence to the throne of grace, so that we may receive mercy and find grace to help in time of need.
>
> Hebrews 4:14–16, NASB

B. Grace is the measure of Christ's gift. And any gift that you have received is a grace-gift. "To each one of us grace was given according to the measure of Christ's gift" (Ephesians 4:7).

C. The will of God will never place you where the grace of God cannot keep you.

Reflection Questions

Lesson 6: Grace Defined

(Answers to these questions can be found in the back of the study guide.)

1. Multiple choice. Fill in the blanks with the best words from this list:
   (a) destiny
   (b) reward
   (c) tutor
   (d) salvation
   Grace is your _____.
   Faith in the completed work of Christ, activated by grace, completes
   your _____.

2. Fill in the blank: If you have truth without _____, you will
   not attract anyone to your message.

3. True or false:
   To the degree that you embrace and receive Christ, you receive grace.

   _____
   Grace and truth are the same thing. _____
   The will of God will never place you where the grace of God cannot
   keep you. _____

4. Referring back to III. A, B and C, list the three requirements for
   grace.
   (a)_____
   (b)_____
   (c)_____

5. Fill in the blanks: "Let us draw near with confidence to the throne of
   grace, so that we may receive _____ and find _____
   to help in time of need" (Hebrews 4:16).

Personal Application Question

6. Write a grace-centered blessing that you can read to yourself as well
   as to others. You can get ideas from the salutations and closings of
   many of Paul's epistles.

LESSON 7

TRANSFORMING FAITH

I. Faith Defined

  A. Faith is a constant, abiding trust in something. Biblically, faith means trust in God ("faith toward God" as our primary study passage, Hebrews 6:1, puts it), not faith in other people or things, in feelings, or in circumstances.

     Faith in God gives us the ability to believe His Word and to appropriate it in our lives. Faith, which comes only after we repent of our self-sufficient trust, does not depend upon the acquisition of information or on prior experience, because it originates in our hearts or spirits rather than in our minds. By faith, we stay connected to the Source of life.

     That is why the Word tells us that "without faith it is impossible to please Him, for he who comes to God must believe that He is, and that He is a rewarder of those who diligently seek Him" (Hebrews 11:6). God is our Father, and He dearly desires to share His life with us. Without faith, we cannot respond to His invitation, which is another way of saying that without faith, we cannot please Him. Without faith, we lack the means to respond to Him.

     We can believe in and have faith in God because of who He is. His Word is true and He Himself is completely incapable of telling a lie. He is trustworthy in the truest sense of the word. Anyone who puts his or her whole trust in Him will not be disappointed.

    1. Hebrews 11:1, NKJV: "Faith is the substance of things hoped for, the evidence of things not seen."

    2. Hebrews 11:1, AMP:

       Now faith is the assurance (the confirmation, the title deed) of the things [we] hope for, being the proof of things [we] do not see and the conviction of their reality [faith perceiving as real fact what is not revealed to the senses].

    2. Hebrews 11:1, NASB: "Faith is the assurance of things hoped for, the conviction of things not seen."

3. Hebrews 11:1, NIV: "Faith is being sure of what we hope for and certain of what we do not see."

B. Two Greek words are translated "faith" in the New Testament:
   1. *Pistis* (noun)
      a. That which causes trust and faith; faithfulness and reliability; solemn promise or oath; proof or pledge
      b. Trust, confidence and faith (in the active sense)
      c. That which is believed (a body of faith or belief, a doctrine)
   2. *Pisteuo* (verb)
      a. To believe in something, to be convinced of something
      b. To trust or believe in God or Christ (with or without a sense of reliance upon God's willingness and ability to help and save)

C. Faith is a *present* reality. Faith is as definite an assurance of the promises of God as a legal title deed. Faith is your contract. Faith states unequivocally, "This is yours. You possess this." *Assurance* in the Greek is the same word used for "reality" or "actual being" (as opposed to what merely seems to be), and also to the realization of something such as a plan.

D. Faith must be contrasted with hope. Hope has to do with waiting for something, while faith does not. Hope is not a present reality. Hope means a desire or an expectation of something in the future. Both hope and faith deal with the realm of the unseen, and they are founded upon God's Word. (See Romans 8:24; 2 Corinthians 5:7. See also Romans 10:17; 15:4.) See how closely faith and hope are connected: "By faith we eagerly await through the Spirit the righteousness for which we hope" (Galatians 5:5, NIV). Without Christ, we can have no such hope (see Ephesians 2:12; 1 Thessalonians 4:13), for hope is rooted in saving faith (see Romans 5:1–5). Hope breeds an atmosphere of faith.

E. Faith is a certainty. Faith looks into the unseen, and it sees things. Faith speaks from the temporal into the eternal, and it calls forth from the eternal realm that which is not yet present in the temporal realm. It pulls eternal reality into your earthly existence. Faith, in other words, is like a magnet, drawing the eternal promises of God into the now.

How can we have such certainty? We can have a solid "conviction of things not seen" because it is based upon the Word of God. "Faith comes by hearing, and hearing by the word of God" (Romans 10:17). Nothing is more certain than that.

   1. Abraham never wavered in believing God's promise. In fact, his faith grew stronger, and in this he brought glory to God. He was fully convinced that God is able to do whatever he promises.

Romans 4:20–21, NLT

2. So shall My word be that goes forth from My mouth;

> It shall not return to Me void,
> But it shall accomplish what I please,
> And it shall prosper in the thing for which I sent it.

Isaiah 55:11

3. God is not a man, that He should lie,

> Nor a son of man, that He should repent.
> Has He said, and will He not do?
> Or has He spoken, and will He not make it good?

Numbers 23:19

F. Faith must be contrasted with sight. Faith is more certain than the things we can see. In fact, "We live by faith, not by sight" (2 Corinthians 5:7, NIV).

1. We fix our eyes not on what is seen, but on what is unseen. For what is seen is temporary, but what is unseen is eternal.

2 Corinthians 4:18, NIV

2. Jesus answered and said to him, "Truly, truly, I say to you, unless one is born again he cannot see the kingdom of God."

John 3:3, NASB

3. I would have lost heart, unless I had believed

> That I would see the goodness of the LORD
> In the land of the living.

Psalm 27:13

4. Jesus said to her, "Did I not say to you that if you would believe you would see the glory of God?"

John 11:40

II. What Causes Faith to Arise?

A. Faith arises by the preaching of the Gospel. In the words of Paul to the Romans: "How then shall they call on Him in whom they have not believed? And how shall they believe in Him of whom they have not heard? And how shall they hear without a preacher?" (Romans 10:14).

1. "At his appointed season he brought his word to light through the preaching entrusted to me by the command of God our Savior" (Titus 1:3, NIV).

2. But what does it say? The Word (God's message in Christ) is near you, on your lips and in your heart; that is, the Word (the message, the basis and object) of faith which we preach.

Romans 10:8, AMP

3. We also [especially] thank God continually for this, that when you received the message of God [which you heard] from us,

you welcomed it not as the word of [mere] men, but as it truly is, the Word of God, which is effectually at work in you who believe [exercising its superhuman power in those who adhere to and trust in and rely on it].

1 Thessalonians 2:13, AMP

  4. "In the beginning was the Word, and the Word was with God, and the Word was God" (John 1:1).

B. Faith arises through the written Word.

  1. On the road to Emmaus (see Luke 24:13–32) after Jesus' death on the cross, the disciples' hearts burned within them as faith burst forth. It happened as they heard the written Word explained to them by the Living Word Himself.

  2. The Word is powerful, and it causes the light of faith to shine. "Your word is a lamp to my feet and a light to my path" (Psalm 119:105).

  3. "When the Jews from Thessalonica learned that the word of God was preached by Paul at Berea, they came there also and stirred up the crowds" (Acts 17:13).

C. Faith arises in times of prayer.

  1. Prayer is two-way communication. When God spoke to Paul, His word built faith in Paul's heart:

He [God] said to me, "My grace is sufficient for you, for My strength is made perfect in weakness." Therefore most gladly I will rather boast in my infirmities, that the power of Christ may rest upon me.

2 Corinthians 12:9

  2. God says, "Before they call, I will answer" (Isaiah 65:24).

  3. God also says, "Call to Me, and I will answer you, and show you great and mighty things, which you do not know" (Jeremiah 33:3).

  4. "Faith comes by hearing, and hearing by the word of God" (Romans 10:17).

D. Faith arises by means of a word of testimony or exhortation.

  1. Faith arose in the heart of the Samaritan woman because of an exhortation: "Come, see a Man who told me all things that I ever did. Could this be the Christ?" (John 4:29).

  2. Let the word of Christ dwell in you richly in all wisdom, teaching and admonishing one another in psalms and hymns and spiritual songs, singing with grace in your hearts to the Lord.

Colossians 3:16

  3. Let us hold fast the confession of our hope without wavering, for He who promised is faithful. And let us consider one another in order to stir up love and good works, not forsaking

the assembling of ourselves together, as is the manner of some, but exhorting one another, and so much the more as you see the Day approaching.

Hebrews 10:23–25

E. Faith arises from dreams, visions and supernatural experiences.
   1. And it shall come to pass in the last days, says God,

   > That I will pour out of My Spirit on all flesh;
   > Your sons and your daughters shall prophesy,
   > Your young men shall see visions,
   > Your old men shall dream dreams.

   Acts 2:17

   2. When Saul was knocked down on the road to Damascus, the extraordinary experience birthed instantaneous faith in his heart. The violent, anti-faith Saul became the faith-filled Saul: "He, trembling and astonished, said, 'Lord, what do You want me to do?'" (Acts 9:6).
   3. Later, when Paul found himself on board a ship in a violent storm, it was the words of an angelic visitor that brought faith-grounded peace to Paul and his fellow travelers (see Acts 27:22–25).
F. Faith arises because of the audible voice of God.
   1. A fresh word from God causes faith to surge up inside us. Consider the effect of the voice from heaven that declared, "This is My beloved Son, in whom I am well pleased" (Matthew 3:17).
   2. Paul's and Ananias's experiences included each of them hearing the audible voice of God (see Acts 9:4–6, 10).
   3. John heard this audible word: "'I am the Alpha and the Omega, the Beginning and the End,' says the Lord, 'who is and who was and who is to come, the Almighty'" (Revelation 1:8).
   4. John heard also:

   > Behold, I am coming quickly! Blessed is he who keeps the words of the prophecy of this book. . . . And behold, I am coming quickly, and My reward is with Me, to give to every one according to his work. I am the Alpha and the Omega, the Beginning and the End, the First and the Last.

   Revelation 22:7, 12–13

III. Adding Faith to the Word
   A. We receive faith from the words of God, and we also base our faith entirely upon what He utters. We treat God's written Word as fact, augmented by His *rhema* (spoken, revelatory) word, and we trust that circumstances will align themselves with the words of God.
   1. A woman who had been hemorrhaging for twelve years had heard about this man Jesus, who could work miracles. Based

on the amazing reports of other people, she brought her own faith for her own situation. After fighting her way through the crowd to get close to Him, she merely touched His garment and she did receive her healing. Jesus turned to her, and said, "Be of good cheer, daughter; your faith has made you well" (Matthew 9:22).

2. Jewish tradition established ways for people to remind themselves of God's words of instruction, so that they would not forget to put their faith in Him (see Numbers 15:38–41). Even though most of us do not wear tassels on our garments to remind us of God's commandments, God's desire remains the same; He wants us to remember His words of instruction so that we can put our faith in them.

B. We look to Abraham, Isaac and other heroes of the faith.

1. By faith Abraham obeyed when he was called to go out to the place which he would receive as an inheritance. And he went out, not knowing where he was going. By faith he dwelt in the land of promise as in a foreign country, dwelling in tents with Isaac and Jacob, the heirs with him of the same promise; for he waited for the city which has foundations, whose builder and maker is God.

By faith Sarah herself also received strength to conceive seed, and she bore a child when she was past the age, because she judged Him faithful who had promised. Therefore from one man, and him as good as dead, were born as many as the stars of the sky in multitude—innumerable as the sand which is by the seashore. . . .

By faith Abraham, when he was tested, offered up Isaac, and he who had received the promises offered up his only begotten son, of whom it was said, "In Isaac your seed shall be called," concluding that God was able to raise him up, even from the dead, from which he also received him in a figurative sense.

Hebrews 11:8–12, 17–19

2. After these things the word of the LORD came to Abram in a vision, saying, "Do not be afraid, Abram. I am your shield, your exceedingly great reward."

But Abram said, "Lord GOD, what will You give me, seeing I go childless, and the heir of my house is Eliezer of Damascus?" Then Abram said, "Look, You have given me no offspring; indeed one born in my house is my heir!"

And behold, the word of the LORD came to him, saying, "This one shall not be your heir, but one who will come from your own body shall be your heir." Then He brought him outside and said, "Look now toward heaven, and count the stars if you are able to number them." And He said to him, "So shall your descendants be."

And he believed in the LORD, and He accounted it to him for righteousness.

Genesis 15:1–6

3. "What does the Scripture say? 'Abraham believed God, and it was accounted to him for righteousness'" (Romans 4:3).
4. But God said to Abraham, "Do not let it be displeasing in your sight because of the lad or because of your bondwoman. Whatever Sarah has said to you, listen to her voice; for in Isaac your seed shall be called. . . ."

Now it came to pass after these things that God tested Abraham, and said to him, "Abraham!"

And he said, "Here I am."

Then He said, "Take now your son, your only son Isaac, whom you love, and go to the land of Moriah, and offer him there as a burnt offering on one of the mountains of which I shall tell you."

Genesis 21:12; 22:1–2

IV. Faith Must Have Action or Expression
A. By faith, Noah moved in the fear of the Lord and built the ark.

By faith Noah, being divinely warned of things not yet seen, moved with godly fear, prepared an ark for the saving of his household, by which he condemned the world and became heir of the righteousness which is according to faith.

Hebrews 11:7

B. Moses' parents entrusted their infant son to another ark made of reeds and released him to float down the river, thus saving him from death and positioning him for his destiny as the leader of the whole people of Israel. (See Exodus 1:22–2:10; Hebrews 11:23.)
C. The lame man was healed when Peter released his faith to reach down and pull him up:

Peter and John went up together to the temple at the hour of prayer, the ninth hour. And a certain man lame from his mother's womb was carried, whom they laid daily at the gate of the temple which is called Beautiful, to ask alms from those who entered the temple; who, seeing Peter and John about to go into the temple, asked for alms. And fixing his eyes on him, with John, Peter said, "Look at us." So he gave them his attention, expecting to receive something from them.

Then Peter said, "Silver and gold I do not have, but what I do have I give you: In the name of Jesus Christ of Nazareth, rise up and walk." And he took him by the right hand and lifted him up, and immediately his feet and ankle bones received strength. So he, leaping up, stood and walked and entered the temple with them—walking, leaping, and praising God.

Acts 3:1–8

D. The woman with the hemorrhage released her faith when she touched Jesus' garment:

> A certain woman had a flow of blood for twelve years, and had suffered many things from many physicians. She had spent all that she had and was no better, but rather grew worse. When she heard about Jesus, she came behind Him in the crowd and touched His garment. For she said, "If only I may touch His clothes, I shall be made well."
>
> Immediately the fountain of her blood was dried up, and she felt in her body that she was healed of the affliction. And Jesus, immediately knowing in Himself that power had gone out of Him, turned around in the crowd and said, "Who touched My clothes?"
>
> But His disciples said to Him, "You see the multitude thronging You, and You say, 'Who touched Me?'"
>
> And He looked around to see her who had done this thing. But the woman, fearing and trembling, knowing what had happened to her, came and fell down before Him and told Him the whole truth. And He said to her, "Daughter, your faith has made you well. Go in peace, and be healed of your affliction."
>
> Mark 5:25–34

V. The Importance of Faith

A. Faith is the fruit of a heart that is open toward God. By faith, we are saved.

1. "By grace you have been saved through faith, and that not of yourselves; it is the gift of God" (Ephesians 2:8).
2. "Since we have been made right in God's sight by faith, we have peace with God because of what Jesus Christ our Lord has done for us" (Romans 5:1, NLT).

B. "The just shall live by faith" (Romans 1:17 and Hebrews 10:38, both quoting Habakkuk 2:4).

C. We are able to keep the faith because we are "kept by faith."

1. "[You] are kept by the power of God through faith for salvation" (1 Peter 1:5).
2. "Every child of God defeats this evil world, and we achieve this victory through our faith" (1 John 5:4, NLT).

D. Enabled by our faith, we are able to defeat the evils of the world, including illness.

1. "The prayer of faith will save the sick, and the Lord will raise him up. And if he has committed sins, he will be forgiven" (James 5:15).
2. "The faith which comes through Him has given him this perfect soundness in the presence of you all" (Acts 3:16).
3. Jesus told the ruler of the synagogue, whose daughter lay on her deathbed, "Do not be afraid; only believe" (Mark 5:36; see also Mark 5:21–24; 35, 37–43).

E. Our faith pleases God more than anything.

    1. "Without faith it is impossible to please Him, for he who comes to God must believe that He is, and that He is a rewarder of those who diligently seek Him" (Hebrews 11:6).

    2. "The angel said to her, 'Rejoice, highly favored one, the Lord is with you; blessed are you among women!' . . . Mary said, 'Behold the maidservant of the Lord! Let it be to me according to your word.'"

Luke 1:28, 38

VI. Living by Faith

A. Faith is not only the way to enter into a life in Christ, but it is also the only way we can continue living that amazing life. Living by faith affects our whole lifestyle, even the food we eat (see, for example, Romans 14). Every time we forget about faith and start relying on our own strength again, we find out the hard way that such a common lapse has consequences. In fact, "Whatever does not originate and proceed from faith is sin" (Romans 14:23, AMP).

B. The person who lives by faith has unlimited potential. "With God all things are possible," Jesus said (Matthew 19:26; see also Mark 9:23). This does not mean that we can do whatever we please, but it does mean that as we seek to live and obey God, we can expect amazing results.

VII. Faith Working through Love

A. Any human effort to obey a code of rules and regulations, to perform religious rituals or even to "be good," minus faith, is wasted. Absolutely nothing we can do can earn us God's approval—with one exception: putting our faith in Him and in the death and resurrection of His Son.

B. Someone who is living by faith will be energized and guided by faith in Jesus. That believer will duplicate His merciful, wise and loving actions.

C. Good works have their place—as evidence of the indwelling Christ. Although we are saved not by good works but rather by grace through faith (see Ephesians 2:8–9; Titus 3:5), our saving faith results in a lifetime of good works (see Ephesians 2:10; Titus 3:7–8). The purpose of God's grace that led us to salvation was to redeem for Himself a people zealous for good works (see Titus 2:11–14).

D. The only thing that counts is "faith expressing itself in love" (Galatians 5:6, NLT).

VIII. Keep It Simple

A. Living by faith, a review: An easy-to-remember principle taken from Mark 11:22–24 is: "Pray until the promise; praise until the provision."

    Step one is to pray until a promise from God's Word becomes a "now," or *rhema* word given by the Holy Spirit. The Spirit may highlight a certain verse of Scripture, or He may speak by means of a spiritual gift (see 1 Corinthians 12:8–10).

Step two is to enter into thanksgiving. The answer is on the way.

B. Keep it simple. Jesus tells each one of His followers, "Do not be afraid; only believe" (Luke 8:50).

Reflection Questions

Lesson 7: Transforming Faith

(Answers to these questions can be found in the back of the study guide.)

1. Fill in the blank:

   We live by faith, not by _____ (see 2 Corinthians 5:7).

   Faith is a present reality, and it must be contrasted with hope. Hope has to do with _____ for something, while faith does not. Hope is not a present reality.

2. Multiple choice: Fill in the blanks with the best words from this list:
   (a) miracles
   (b) warfare
   (c) potential
   (d) words

   We must base our faith entirely on the _____ of God.

   The person who lives by faith has unlimited _____.

3. True or false:

   It is impossible to please God without faith. ____

   Faith not only gives us entrance into life in Christ, but it is also the only way we can continue to walk with Him. ____

4. Faith arises through (See Section II of lesson 7.)

   1. _____
   2. _____
   3. _____
   4. _____
   5. _____
   6. _____

5. (Refer to section VII. C. to fill in the blanks.) Although we are saved not by _____ _____ but rather by grace through faith (see Ephesians 2:8–9; Titus 3:5), our saving faith results in a lifetime of _____ _____ (see Ephesians 2:10; Titus 3:7–8). The purpose of God's grace that led us to salvation was to redeem

for Himself a people zealous for _____ _____ (see Titus 2:11–14).

Personal Application Question

6. Another word for *faith* is *trust*. Read all of Hebrews 11. Each time you see the word *faith*, replace it with the word *trust*. Ask the Holy Spirit to enrich your understanding of what faith in God is. Write down any ways that you see faith differently.

LESSON 8

VITAL: WATER BAPTISM

I. Baptism Defined

   A. As the initiatory rite for the Church of Jesus Christ, water baptism always involves three aspects: (1) a subject, one who baptizes; (2) an object, one who is being baptized; and (3) an element into which those who are being baptized are immersed. The word *baptize* originated from a root word that meant "to dip," which, sometimes further connoted "to wash." A true baptism (historically, Christians do not agree on this) must involve more than sprinkling or pouring. The object of the baptism must become wet, having been dipped down and completely covered in water—total immersion.

     The Old Testament precursor of Christian water baptism could be found wherever water or some equivalent of water was being administered, whether by other people, natural elements or miracles. So we see a foreshadowing of baptism in the crossing of the Red Sea, to which Paul referred specifically: "They were all baptized into Moses in the cloud and in the sea" (1 Corinthians 10:2, NIV; see also Exodus 14). The cloud is like the Holy Spirit, and the Red Sea is like the waters of death, burial and resurrection.

     To explain how God purges the filth of the flesh, Peter profiles the example of Noah, portraying not only the picture of baptism provided by the Flood, but also the blood atonement of Jesus Christ as the prerequisite to being totally immersed in the will and the purposes of God:

> Christ suffered for our sins once for all time. He never sinned, but he died for sinners to bring you safely home to God. He suffered physical death, but he was raised to life in the Spirit.
>
> So he went and preached to the spirits in prison—those who disobeyed God long ago when God waited patiently while Noah was building his boat. Only eight people were saved from drowning in

that terrible flood. And that water is a picture of baptism, which now saves you, not by removing dirt from your body, but as a response to God from a clean conscience. It is effective because of the resurrection of Jesus Christ.

1 Peter 3:18–21, NLT

B. Explore Greek New Testament terms for baptism.
   1. Noun forms: (1) *baptisma* (found only in the New Testament), refers to immersion in water in the accounts of John's baptism in Matthew, Mark, Luke and Acts and in accounts of Christian baptism. (See Romans 6:4; Ephesians 4:5; 1 Peter 3:21; and in some manuscripts, Colossians 2:12.) The same word has also been used in a figurative sense, describing immersion in martyrdom or suffering. (See Mark 10:38–39; Luke 12:50; Matthew 20:22–23.) (2) *baptismos* refers to the baptisms (immersion, dipping or washings) of the Mosaic Law, the washing of dishes or ritual washings. In context, that word tends to be used as a contrast to Christian baptism. (It is used in Mark 7:4, 8; Hebrews 6:2; 9:10; and the preferred reading of Colossians 2:12.)
   2. Verb form: *baptizo,* translated "dip," "immerse," "plunge," "wash," "drench," "overwhelm," "sink" and "submerge." An intensive form of the verb means Christian baptism, martyrdom and Jewish ritual washings, as well as Israel's deliverance through the Red Sea and being baptized in the Holy Spirit ("and fire"—see Matthew 3:11 and Luke 3:16).
C. Throughout both the Old and New Testaments, we can find about eighty different dipping-related applications of the verb *baptize.* See, for example, Luke 16:24 (the parable of the rich man asking to have the beggar Lazarus quench his thirst by dipping his finger in water), John 13:26 (a piece of bread, dipped in wine) and Revelation 19:13 (Jesus' robe, dipped in blood). The phrase "baptism in the Holy Spirit" never occurs in the New Testament, but the verb form "baptized in the Spirit" speaks of the reality of being immersed in God's Holy Spirit.

The immersion factor is denoted by the Greek preposition *en* ("in," "with" or "by") and the purpose of the immersion is indicated by the Greek preposition *eis,* which means "into." In overview, we see the following:
1. John's baptism (see Matthew 3:5–11).
2. Christian believers' baptisms (see Matthew 28:19; Acts 2:38; Romans 6:3–4; Galatians 3:27).
3. Baptism in the Holy Spirit (see Matthew 3:11; Mark 1:8; Luke 3:16).
4. Typological baptism (see 1 Corinthians 10:1–2).
5. Metaphorical (suffering) baptism (see Mark 10:38–39; Luke 12:49–50).

II. Who Is Eligible for Water Baptism?

A. New converts need to be taught the truth about water baptism.

In the New Testament, a baptism demonstrated an informed decision on the part of the one being baptized. The person was making a public statement: "I receive Christ as Savior and Lord." It did not represent an intention to make such a decision in the future, nor was it like signing up for church membership or a catechism class.

Baptism figures prominently in Jesus' Great Commission to His disciples: "Go therefore and make disciples of all the nations, baptizing them in the name of the Father and of the Son and of the Holy Spirit" (Matthew 28:19).

New Testament believers were baptized as soon as it was feasible after they first believed (see Mark 16:16). Examples abound:

1. The Jews at Pentecost:

> With many other words he testified and exhorted them, saying, "Be saved from this perverse generation." Then those who gladly received his word were *baptized;* and that day about three thousand souls were added to them.
>
> Acts 2:40–41, emphasis added

2. The Samaritan believers:

> When they believed Philip as he preached the things concerning the kingdom of God and the name of Jesus Christ, both men and women were *baptized.*
>
> Acts 8:12, emphasis added

3. The Ethiopian eunuch:

> The eunuch answered Philip and said, "I ask you, of whom does the prophet say this, of himself or of some other man?" Then Philip opened his mouth, and beginning at this Scripture, preached Jesus to him. Now as they went down the road, they came to some water. And the eunuch said, "See, here is water. What hinders me from being *baptized?*"
>
> Then Philip said, "If you believe with all your heart, you may."
> And he answered and said, "I believe that Jesus Christ is the Son of God." So he commanded the chariot to stand still. And both Philip and the eunuch went down into the water, and he *baptized* him.
>
> Acts 8:34–38, emphasis added

4. Saul/Paul:

> Ananias departed and entered the house, and after laying his hands on him said, "Brother Saul, the Lord Jesus, who appeared to you on the road by which you were coming, has sent me so that you may regain your sight and be filled with the Holy Spirit."

And immediately there fell from his eyes something like scales, and he regained his sight, and he got up and was *baptized*; and he took food and was strengthened.

Acts 9:17–19, NASB, emphasis added

5. The Philippian jailer:

He brought them out and said, "Sirs, what must I do to be saved?"

So they said, "Believe on the Lord Jesus Christ, and you will be saved, you and your household." Then they spoke the word of the Lord to him and to all who were in his house. And he took them the same hour of the night and washed their stripes. *And immediately he and all his family were baptized.*

Acts 16:30–33, emphasis added

B. Repentance must be demonstrated in the life of the believer.

Not undertaken lightly, baptism was for new converts who had demonstrated sincere repentance prior to being baptized. Nowhere does the Bible teach that there is some kind of baptismal regeneration that completes the salvation process, but rather that baptism is the seal of assurance of the inner work of the Spirit.

Then, as now, without a significant change of lifestyle and confession of sin, a candidate for water baptism will only go under the water as a dry sinner and come up a wet one. Only through faith in the finished work of Calvary and through the power of the Holy Spirit within can someone be truly born again.

Baptism is the entryway into the full Christian life:

"Peter said to them, 'Repent, and let every one of you be baptized in the name of Jesus Christ for the remission of sins; and you shall receive the gift of the Holy Spirit'" (Acts 2:38; see also Romans 6:3–4).

C. A new believer hears and obeys the Word of God.

In all of these examples, the Spirit of God touched the hearts of the hearers when the Word of God was being declared and then their faith rose to a level that brought them to action. As soon as the Good News became clear to people, requesting and receiving baptism was their response, whether this was almost instantaneous, as in the case of the Ethiopian eunuch, or after a lapse of years, as in the case of the Ephesian believers in Acts 19:5. This is a perfect example of faith being demonstrated by an action.

D. A new believer puts faith in the finished work of Calvary. Early or late, the believer will recognize the effectiveness of Jesus' death on the cross. He or she will understand that the finished work of Calvary means much more than having an escape hatch from hell or a crutch to lean on as a last resort in moments of anguish. Baptism will be the next logical step. (See Mark 16:16 and Acts 8:12, 36–37.)

III. What Happens to a Believer upon Baptism?

A. New Testament believers become children of Abraham.

Baptism is to the Christian what circumcision is to the Jewish people. Just as circumcision signified complete agreement with God's covenant with the people of Israel, so water baptism signifies full surrender to the Lord, representing the relinquishment of all rights to ourselves. In a divine continuum, it also indicates that the newly baptized person has become one of the children of Abraham. Grafted into the people of God, even non-Jews become recipients of all of the promises of God. (See Genesis 12:1–3; 17:3–4, 7 for God's original promises to Abraham, reiterated and coupled with circumcision in Genesis 17:9–14.)

The apostle Paul, himself a zealous Jew who had been "circumcised on the eighth day" (see Philippians 3:5), put it this way:

> All who have been united with Christ in baptism have put on Christ, like putting on new clothes. There is no longer Jew or Gentile, slave or free, male and female. For you are all one in Christ Jesus. And now that you belong to Christ, you are the true children of Abraham. You are his heirs, and God's promise to Abraham belongs to you.
>
> Galatians 3:27–29, NLT

B. Baptism is a circumcision of the heart, not the flesh. Baptism effects an invisible operation on "the foreskin of your heart" (Deuteronomy 10:16). Baptism makes it official; a person's soul and spirit have been changed; from that point forward, the person can be said to have a "circumcised heart." His or her "body of flesh" or "old nature" or "body of sin" has been removed.

Water baptism is not just a ritual in the Church, it is a work of the Holy Spirit that testifies to the fact that "I [the Lord] will be to them a God, and they shall be to me a people" (Hebrews 8:10, KJV). Baptism proves a love bond—an identification with Jesus' death. Out of love, we want to die with Him (see Deuteronomy 30:5–6). God has completed the connection. As the apostle Paul explained it to two different groups of people:

> You are not a true Jew just because you were born of Jewish parents or because you have gone through the ceremony of circumcision. No, a true Jew is one whose heart is right with God. And true circumcision is not merely obeying the letter of the law; rather, it is a change of heart produced by God's Spirit. And a person with a changed heart seeks praise from God, not from people.
>
> Romans 2:28–29, NLT

In Him you were also circumcised with the circumcision made without hands, by putting off the body of the sins of the flesh, by the circumcision of Christ, buried with Him in baptism, in which you also were raised with Him through faith in the working of God, who raised Him from the dead.

Colossians 2:11–12

C. We have been baptized into both Jesus' death and His life. Buried in the waters of baptism, believers rise up to new life. "As many of us as were baptized into Christ Jesus were baptized into His death" (Romans 6:3), signifying full acceptance of the death and burial of Jesus as it applies personally. Baptism is an acknowledgment of one's own death in Christ and one's resurrection to new life. This life is like an inheritance—disbursed only after death. He had to die to make it available. We have to die to receive it.

IV. Reasons to Be Baptized

A. Jesus commanded that His followers be baptized and that they baptize others: "Go therefore and make disciples of all the nations, baptizing them in the name of the Father and of the Son and of the Holy Spirit" (Matthew 28:19).

B. Jesus Himself sought baptism from His cousin John, thus giving us an example to follow: "Jesus came from Galilee to John at the Jordan to be baptized by him" (Matthew 3:13).

C. Baptism demonstrates that those who have been baptized have a clear conscience toward God:

That water [the Flood] is a picture of baptism, which now saves you, not by removing dirt from your body, but as a response to God from a clean conscience. It is effective because of the resurrection of Jesus Christ.

1 Peter 3:21, NLT

D. Each baptism testifies to the death, burial and resurrection of the Lord Jesus Christ:

As many of us as were baptized into Christ Jesus were baptized into His death[.] Therefore we were buried with Him through baptism into death, that just as Christ was raised from the dead by the glory of the Father, even so we also should walk in newness of life. For if we have been united together in the likeness of His death, certainly we also shall be in the likeness of His resurrection, knowing this, that our old man was crucified with Him, that the body of sin might be done away with, that we should no longer be slaves of sin. For he who has died has been freed from sin.

Romans 6:3–7

E. Each baptism testifies to the defeat of Satan:

In Him you were also . . . buried with Him in baptism, in which you also were raised with Him through faith in the working of God, who raised Him from the dead. . . . Having disarmed principalities and powers, He made a public spectacle of them, triumphing over them in it.

Colossians 2:11–12, 15 (see also Colossians 1:21–22)

F. When a person gets baptized, the event becomes a public confession of that person's faith and fellowship within the Body of Christ (see Matthew 10:32; Acts 2:41; Galatians 3:26–28).

G. Baptism provides the avenue for walking in newness of life:

We were buried with Him through baptism into death, that just as Christ was raised from the dead by the glory of the Father, even so we also should walk in newness of life.

Romans 6:4

H. Baptism proves to be a multi-faceted witness; for example:
1. A witness to the world ("My sinful nature has been crucified and I intend to bury it forever. I am dead to the world of sin.")
2. A witness to the Christian family ("I identify myself with you and I join you.")
3. A witness to God ("I come out from the kingdom of darkness and into Your Kingdom.")
4. A witness to ourselves ("I willingly enter into death, burial and resurrection, identifying myself with my Savior Jesus. My life is now hid with Christ in God. I must no longer live for myself but for the One who redeemed me.")

V. Baptism and Conversion
A. Both Jesus and the apostle Peter included baptism as part of the appropriate response to hearing the Gospel message (see Matthew 28:19 and Acts 2:38).

People wonder if that means people need to be baptized in order to get into heaven. Remember the repentant thief on the cross next to Jesus (see Luke 23:39–43). He was accepted into heaven, having responded with repentant faith in the last moments of his life and yet having no opportunity to be baptized.

In most cases, people should seek their earliest opportunity to be baptized, as the Ethiopian eunuch did. He said to Philip, who had just persuaded him of the Gospel message, "Look, here is water. Why shouldn't I be baptized?" (Acts 8:36, NIV).

Baptism is not an absolute requirement for getting into heaven, but neither is it optional. After all, Jesus Himself, who clearly did not need to be baptized to prove repentance from sin or to be admitted to heaven, submitted to being water baptized "to fulfill all righteousness" (Matthew 3:15), setting an example for everyone to follow.

B. "Repent and . . . be baptized" (Acts 2:38). Baptism is ineffectual without sincere repentance on the part of the person being baptized. For this reason, children born into a Christian family need to receive the Gospel and repent at some point, making a personal decision to follow Christ. This, in the opinion of many, brings the tradition of infant baptism into question.

Proponents often cite the household conversions that were followed by household baptisms (see Acts 10:30–48 and 16:29–34), but in such cases the ones who were saved were able to respond to the preaching of the Gospel, so those households must not have included infants.

Still, the Bible has not mandated a minimum age for baptism. Some Christian traditions will not baptize children younger than twelve or thirteen, which is considered the age of accountability. Yet nothing in the New Testament prohibits baptism for toddlers who understand the Gospel and repent.

In baptism, the person's age, the status of the person administering baptism, and the location, creeds and ceremony involved take second place to the primary qualifications of repentance and faith.

C. In whose name should people be baptized? Jesus said, "Go therefore and make disciples of all the nations, baptizing them in the name of the Father and of the Son and of the Holy Spirit" (Matthew 28:19). This has become the formulaic wording for baptisms ever since, although the early Church baptized new converts "in the name of the Lord Jesus" (Acts 19:5 and elsewhere) without mentioning the Father and the Holy Spirit.

To baptize in the name of Jesus expresses the reality of the fact that in baptism we come into a close unity with God, and that, in fact, we pass into His ownership. Being baptized in the name of the Lord Jesus is the same as being baptized in the name of the Father, the Son Jesus and the Holy Spirit. Early candidates for baptism were conscious of being sealed into an intimate relationship with their Lord Jesus. For example: "As many of you as were baptized into Christ have put on Christ" (Galatians 3:27), and "Do you not know that as many of us as were baptized into Christ Jesus were baptized into His death?" (Romans 6:3). Combining both the gospel accounts and the book of Acts, most of the Church today baptizes in the name of the Father God, the Son Jesus and the Holy Spirit.

D. Baptism honors each member of the triune God. In the Father, we receive new birth and life as a son or daughter and put on the nature of Jesus His Son (see Galatians 3:26–27; 4:6–7). In the name of the Son, we share in the forgiveness of sins (see Ephesians 1:7; 2:8; Colossians 2:11–12). In the name of the Spirit, we gain indwelling and spiritual strength (see Acts 1:8; Ephesians 3:16).

Reflection Questions

Lesson 8: Vital: Water Baptism

(Answers to these questions can be found in the back of the study guide.)

1. Multiple choice: Insert the best word in the blanks:
    (a) immerse
    (b) repent
    (c) circumcise
    Unless people truly _____, they go under the
       baptismal water as a dry sinner, and come up as a wet one.
    Baptism means to _____ one's heart.
    To baptize means to completely _____.

2. Referring to section IV. A.–H., list eight reasons to be baptized:
    (1)_____
    (2)_____
    (3)_____
    (4)_____
    (5)_____
    (6)_____
    (7)_____
    (8)_____

3. True or false:
    When believers get baptized, they become children of Abraham. _____
    Baptism is the entryway into the full Christian life, complete with
       the indwelling Holy Spirit. _____

4. Fill in the blanks: In the name of the _____, we receive new
    birth and life as a son or daughter and put on the nature of Jesus. In
    the name of the _____, we share in the forgiveness of sins.
    In the name of the _____ _____, we gain indwelling
    and spiritual renewal.

5. Fill in the blanks: Believers are baptized into both Jesus' _____ and His life. _____ in the waters of baptism, believers rise up to new life.

Personal Application Question

6. Have you yourself received baptism in water since becoming a believer? If your answer is "no" or "I'm not sure," what do you plan to do about it? If your answer is "yes," what do you remember about the occasion? Could you tell any difference in yourself afterward? What did you notice? If you could not discern any differences, does this invalidate your baptism? Why or why not?

LESSON 9

THE GLORIOUS BAPTISM IN THE HOLY SPIRIT

I. **The One Called Alongside to Help**

   A. When Jesus was preparing His disciples for His imminent crucifixion, He comforted them by promising that He would send "another" to be with them after His departure:

   > I will pray the Father, and He will give you another Helper, that He may abide with you forever—the Spirit of truth, whom the world cannot receive, because it neither sees Him nor knows Him; but you know Him, for He dwells with you and will be in you.
   >
   > John 14:16–17

   B. The Spirit of truth, also known as the Holy Spirit, would keep them close to God. In Greek, He was known as *parakletos* (anglicized to *paraclete*), meaning "one called alongside to help." (See John 14:15–26; 15:26; 16:5–15.)

   C. The promised Holy Spirit would help in many ways.

   1. He would stay forever.

   2. He would dwell in believers.

   3. He would teach believers all things.

   4. He would bring the words of Jesus to remembrance.

   5. He would bear witness of Jesus.

   6. He would convict the world.

   7. He would guide believers into all truth.

   8. He would glorify Jesus.

   9. He would give us power.

   D. Water baptism is meant to be the doorway to the life-changing experience of being baptized in the Holy Spirit. Just as water baptism is not an absolute requirement for getting into heaven (although this does not render it optional), baptism in the Spirit is not required for salvation, either. Without being baptized in the Spirit, however, no one can live an abundant and fully supernatural Christian life.

II. **The Nature of the Holy Spirit**

   A. The Holy Spirit is the third expression of the Godhead.

1. The Holy Spirit is not a mere influence or power. He is the third personality of the triune Godhead. (See 1 John 5:6–8.)

2. He is a person, One who can do all of the following, like a human person:

   a. He *speaks* (see Acts 13:2).

   b. He *works* (see 1 Corinthians 12:11).

   c. He *teaches* (see John 14:26).

   d. He *guides* (see John 16:13).

3. In common with any personality, the Holy Spirit shares the following characteristics:

   a. He has a *mind*—"He who searches the hearts knows what the mind of the Spirit is" (Romans 8:27).

   b. He has a *will*—"One and the same Spirit works all these things, distributing to each one individually as He wills" (1 Corinthians 12:11).

   c. He has *intelligence*—"You also gave Your good Spirit to instruct them" (Nehemiah 9:20).

   d. He expresses *love*—"I beg you, brethren, through the Lord Jesus Christ, and through the love of the Spirit . . ." (Romans 15:30; see also Galatians 5:22; Colossians 1:8).

   e. He also expresses *grief*—"Do not grieve the Holy Spirit of God" (Ephesians 4:30).

B. Although He is a Person, He remains invisible. Therefore one of the best ways to refer to Him is through metaphorical symbols. In Scripture, the Holy Spirit is known in the following ways:

   1. *Dove* (See Matthew 3:16.)

   2. *Water* (See John 4:14; 7:38–39.)

   3. *Rain* (See Joel 2:23.)

   4. *Oil* (See Psalm 89:20.)

   5. *Wind* (See John 3:8; Acts 2:2.)

   6. *Fire* (See Isaiah 4:4; Luke 3:16; Acts 2:3.)

C. He is also known by a number of names, each of which helps to portray an aspect of His personality:

   1. The Spirit of the Lord; The Spirit of Wisdom and Understanding; The Spirit of Counsel and Might; The Spirit of Knowledge and of the Fear of the Lord (all found in Isaiah 11:2).

   2. The Spirit of Christ (See 1 Peter 1:11.)

   3. The Spirit of Prophecy (See Revelation 19:10.)

   4. The Spirit of Glory (See 1 Peter 4:14.)

   5. The Comforter (See John 14:26.)

   6. The Eternal Spirit (See Hebrews 9:14.)

   7. The Spirit of Promise (See Ephesians 1:13.)

III. Biblical History Regarding the Baptism in the Holy Spirit

A. The outpouring of the Holy Spirit was long predicted by Old Testament prophets, so when it occurred on the Day of Pentecost after Jesus' ascension, those present recognized it not only as a fulfillment of what their ascended Lord had just told them, but also of centuries-old predictions.

1. I will pour water on him who is thirsty,

> And floods on the dry ground;
> I will pour My Spirit on your descendants,
> And My blessing on your offspring.

Isaiah 44:3

2. I will give you a new heart and put a new spirit within you; I will take the heart of stone out of your flesh and give you a heart of flesh.

Ezekiel 36:26

3. It shall come to pass afterward

> That I will pour out My Spirit on all flesh;
> Your sons and your daughters shall prophesy,
> Your old men shall dream dreams,
> Your young men shall see visions.
> And also on My menservants and on My maidservants
> I will pour out My Spirit in those days.

Joel 2:28–29

4. I will pour on the house of David and on the inhabitants of Jerusalem the Spirit of grace and supplication; then they will look on Me whom they pierced. Yes, they will mourn for Him as one mourns for his only son, and grieve for Him as one grieves for a firstborn.

Zechariah 12:10

B. New Testament prophets and disciples testified regarding the Holy Spirit baptism.

1. John the Baptist had pointed toward a coming baptism of the Spirit, saying, "I indeed baptized you with water, but He will baptize you with the Holy Spirit" (Mark 1:8).

2. Jesus commanded His followers to wait in Jerusalem until they received "power from on high" (Luke 24:49). Their resurrected Lord left no doubt that He was referring to the fulfillment of the long-awaited "Promise of the Father" (Acts 1:4). Jesus spoke of it as being "baptized with the Holy Spirit not many days from now" (Acts 1:5).

3. Peter recognized the promise of the Holy Spirit on the Day of Pentecost: "Now he [Jesus] is exalted to the place of highest honor in heaven, at God's right hand. And the Father, as he had promised, gave him the Holy Spirit to pour out upon us, just as you see and hear today" (Acts 2:33, NLT).

C. The Holy Spirit has been promised to the Church of all ages. In spite of having had such a long prophetic history, the outpouring of the Holy Spirit on the Day of Pentecost would have become a footnote in the annals of the people of God if it had not continued up to the present day. Peter recognized its significance immediately, and he boldly declared:

1. You shall receive the gift of the Holy Spirit. For the promise is to you and to your children, and to all who are afar off, as many as the Lord our God will call.

Acts 2:38–39

2. The promise was meant for those who were present that day ("you").
3. The promise was meant for their sons and daughters ("your children").
4. The promise was meant for all believers in Jesus in any land and in any future timeframe ("to all who are afar off").

IV. **Key Accounts in the Book of Acts**

A. The New Testament believers encountered the Holy Spirit in such a strong way that they were spoken of as being *baptized,* or immersed, in Him. This terminology had been used earlier by Jesus and also by His forerunner, John the Baptist, who stated it so clearly that it was recorded in all four gospel accounts:

I indeed baptize you with water unto repentance, but He who is coming after me is mightier than I, whose sandals I am not worthy to carry. He will baptize you with the Holy Spirit and fire.

Matthew 3:11

I indeed baptized you with water, but He will baptize you with the Holy Spirit.

Mark 1:8

I indeed baptize you with water; but One mightier than I is coming, whose sandal strap I am not worthy to loose. He will baptize you with the Holy Spirit and fire.

Luke 3:16

I did not know Him, but He who sent me to baptize with water said to me, "Upon whom you see the Spirit descending, and remaining on Him, this is He who baptizes with the Holy Spirit."

John 1:33

B. The Holy Spirit came on the Day of Pentecost. Jesus had instructed the apostles and other disciples to wait for the promised Holy Spirit (see Acts 1:4–5, 8). They waited together for weeks in an upper room in Jerusalem. Suddenly, it happened:

When the Day of Pentecost had fully come, they were all with one accord in one place. And suddenly there came a sound from heaven, as of a rushing mighty wind, and it filled the whole house where they were sitting. Then there appeared to them divided tongues, as of fire, and one sat upon each of them. And they were all filled with the Holy Spirit and began to speak with other tongues, as the Spirit gave them utterance.

Acts 2:1–4

He came with a sound like a windstorm. Visible flames appeared above each person's head. Out of their astonished mouths came a cacophony of languages—a *loud* babble of tongues, noisy enough to attract an immediate crowd, some of whom thought that a drunken party must have just spilled out into the street (see Acts 2:1–13).

The believers, who had already been individually born again, were now "born" again as the Church of Jesus Christ, gifted and empowered by His own Spirit. The hearts of the bystanders were pierced with conviction. By the end of the day, the apostles had been joined by and had baptized three thousand new believers (see Acts 2:41).

C. The same Spirit was poured out on the Samaritan believers.

The apostles traveled from place to place, preaching and teaching, as guided by the Spirit (see Acts 8:1). Philip preached the Gospel in the city of Samaria, with miracles of healing and deliverance from evil spirits (see Acts 8:5–7). The hearts of both men and women were filled with faith and they received baptism in water (see Acts 8:12), but none of the new converts had yet received the fullness of the Spirit. Peter and John came to join Philip, as none of the new converts had yet received the fullness of the Spirit (see Acts 8:14–16). The apostles laid their hands on them, and the new believers received the Holy Spirit (see Acts 8:17). Jesus' words were coming true: "You will receive power . . . and you will be my witnesses in Jerusalem . . . and Samaria" (Acts 1:8, NIV).

D. The Spirit arrested Saul on the road to Damascus. Saul, who had persecuted the believers mercilessly, was converted dramatically, then healed and filled with the Spirit. Saul (soon renamed Paul) was first baptized in the Spirit, and shortly afterward he was baptized in water, in the opposite order from most people. The gifts of the Spirit became wonderfully evident in Paul's life, including the gift of tongues (see 1 Corinthians 14:18).

E. The Spirit filled the new Gentile believers just as He had filled the Jewish believers. In a vision during a rooftop trance, Peter was led to preach the Gospel to Cornelius's houseful of Gentiles (see Acts 10 and 11). All of them received the gift of tongues as the Spirit fell while Philip was speaking (see Acts 10:44–46). Their initial conversion was nearly simultaneous with their baptism in the Holy Spirit, and water baptism soon followed (see Acts 10:47–48).

F. Paul found a dozen Ephesian disciples who had been born again, but who had never heard of the Holy Spirit, nor had they been water baptized except with John's baptism of repentance (see Acts 19:1–7). Soon they had been water baptized and baptized in the Spirit with the evidence of speaking in tongues.

This account shows that a person can be a valid disciple and yet not be enlightened to the realities of the Spirit, and that a person might come progressively into these stages of spiritual liberty.

V. Authority and Power

A. The main purpose for receiving the baptism in the Holy Spirit is that we might receive power. Our new birth brought us *exousia,* the authority and power to become the children of God, with a right to the inheritance of our Father (see Romans 8:14–17 and Ephesians 1).

The baptism in the Spirit brings us into *dunamis,* the power to live as children of God (see Acts 1:8), including, according to the Greek lexicon (Strong's #1411), the "power for performing miracles" and resident "moral power and excellence of soul."

The new birth gives us the right to be God's children, while the baptism in the Holy Spirit brings us power to live effective lives as God's children.

B. Common "power" manifestations of the baptism in the Holy Spirit include the following:

1. The boldness to testify about Christ.
2. "Drunkenness" in the Spirit.
3. The appearance or the feeling of the fire of God.
4. The fruit of the Spirit ("love, joy, peace, longsuffering, kindness, goodness, faithfulness, gentleness, and self-control," according to Galatians 5:22–23).
5. Increasing truth, light and revelation.
6. Greater conviction.
7. Gifts of the Spirit, including the gift of tongues.

C. The baptism in the Holy Spirit is both an outward and an inward experience available to everyone.

1. Outwardly, the invisible presence and power of the Holy Spirit comes down from above and believers are surrounded or immersed in it.
2. Inwardly, believers drink in the Holy Spirit like water until they are filled, eventually overflowing as though a river were pouring from their innermost being.

D. The outward evidence of the baptism in the Spirit is most commonly the gift of tongues.

1. Speaking in tongues was the evidence by which the apostles themselves received the Spirit.
2. Thus, this was the evidence the apostles accepted as validation of the experience of others.
3. The apostles never asked for any alternative confirmation.

4. No alternative evidence is ever offered to us in the New Testament.

VI. How Does the Believer Receive the Baptism of the Holy Spirit?

    A. The Spirit is imparted as a sovereign act of God (see Acts 2:2–4 and Acts 10:44–46). Note, however, that we always see a coupling of Holy Spirit initiative and human response.

    B. Most commonly, the recipient relies on another believer who has already received the Spirit to pray with the laying on of hands. This was true in the early Church and it remains true today, although the temptation has been strong to abuse such a simple method (see, for example, the account of Simon the magician in Acts 8:14–19).

    C. The human response should be simply to *ask* in faith.

        1. We must believe it is God's personal promise for today (see Acts 2:39).

        2. We must prepare our hearts through repentance (see Acts 2:38).

        3. We must ask: "If you then, being evil, know how to give good gifts to your children, how much more will your heavenly Father give the Holy Spirit to those who ask Him!" (Luke 11:13).

        4. We must receive what He gives us. (See John 7:38–39 and Galatians 3:2.)

VII. The Benefits of Receiving

    A. *Edification.* Scripturally and experientially, the personal benefits of being baptized in the Holy Spirit make it possible for a believer to participate fully in the Kingdom ministry of Jesus on the earth. Through His Spirit dwelling in your heart, you will be built up in your faith, or edified:

> Dear friends, build yourselves up in your most holy faith and pray in the Holy Spirit. Keep yourselves in God's love as you wait for the mercy of our Lord Jesus Christ to bring you to eternal life.
>
> Jude 20–21, NIV

> The Spirit helps us in our weakness. We do not know what we ought to pray for, but the Spirit himself intercedes for us with groans that words cannot express. And he who searches our hearts knows the mind of the Spirit, because the Spirit intercedes for the saints in accordance with God's will.
>
> Romans 8:26–27, NIV

> One who speaks in a tongue edifies himself; but one who prophesies edifies the church.
>
> 1 Corinthians 14:4, NASB

    B. *Effectiveness as a witness.* With the combination of the guidance, wisdom and breakthrough power of the Holy Spirit, you will be able to become an effective witness to the truth of the Good News of Jesus Christ. (See Acts 1:8.)

C. *Increase in the fruit of the Spirit.* Generations of believers can testify to ever-growing maturity and a lifelong increase in the fruit of the Spirit (see Galatians 5:22–23).

D. *Personal transformation.* Even the most concerted human effort cannot produce the level of personal transformation that the Holy Spirit can effect in your life:

> He saved us, not on the basis of deeds which we have done in righteousness, but according to His mercy, by the washing of regeneration and renewing by the Holy Spirit, whom He poured out upon us richly through Jesus Christ our Savior.
>
> Titus 3:5–6, NASB

> We, who with unveiled faces all reflect the Lord's glory, are being transformed into his likeness with ever-increasing glory, which comes from the Lord, who is the Spirit.
>
> 2 Corinthians 3:18, NIV

E. When we are baptized in the Holy Spirit, the Helper comes to us, as promised, to equip us every day, to enlighten us, to clothe us with power from on high. If we did not love God before, we will be able to love Him now, because He who *is* love now lives in us.

Reflection Questions

Lesson 9: The Glorious: Baptism in the Holy Spirit

(Answers to these questions can be found in the back of the study guide.)

1. True or false:

    The ministry of Christ is to baptize the believer in the Holy Spirit.
    _____

    The baptism of the Holy Spirit is a prerequisite for getting into heaven. _____

    The baptism of the Holy Spirit is a distinct experience from salvation and water baptism. _____

2. The Holy Spirit, also known as the Helper, helps us in many ways. List several of the ways He helps. (See section I. C.)

    _____

    _____

    _____

    _____

    _____

3. What do the following things have in common: fire, water, rain, oil, wind and a dove? _____

    _____

4. Fill in the blanks:

    I will give you a new _____ and put a new _____ within you; I will take the _____ of stone out of your flesh and give you a _____ of flesh.

    Ezekiel 36:26

5. Multiple choice: Choose the best word for each blank:

    (a) fruit

    (b) power

    (c) transformation

The main purpose for receiving the baptism in the Holy Spirit is that we might receive _____.

Generations of believers can testify to ever-growing maturity and a lifelong increase in the _____ of the Spirit.

Even the most concerted human effort cannot produce the level of personal _____ that the Holy Spirit can effect in your life.

Personal Application Question

6. Have you yourself received the Holy Spirit since you believed in Jesus? How can you be sure? Have you ever prayed for someone else to receive the Holy Spirit? What were the results of your prayer?

LESSON 10

WITH THESE HANDS

I. Principle in Practice

   A. The laying on of hands links heaven and earth. One person's hands are placed upon another person for the purpose of releasing specific spiritual blessings, often accompanied by prayer or various forms of prophetic utterance. These hands release loving blessing, consecration, miracles and spiritual gifts. Paul laid his hands on his protégé, Timothy, as we know from this familiar passage:

> I remind you to stir up the gift of God which is in you through the laying on of my hands. For God has not given us a spirit of fear, but of power and of love and of a sound mind.
>
> 2 Timothy 1:6–7

   B. Why devote an entire lesson to the laying on of hands? The topic has been included because it is one of the fundamentals mentioned in the theme Scripture of this entire study:

> Let us stop going over the basic teachings about Christ again and again. Let us go on instead and become mature in our understanding. Surely we don't need to start again with the fundamental importance of repenting from evil deeds and placing our faith in God. You don't need further instruction about baptisms, *the laying on of hands,* the resurrection of the dead, and eternal judgment.
>
> Hebrews 6:1–2, NLT (emphasis added)

   C. The ordinance of the laying on of hands is clearly associated with ministering the baptism in the Holy Spirit, imparting spiritual gifts, ministering healing and deliverance, releasing consecration and blessing, and setting apart both local and trans-local church ministries.

II. Three Old Testament Precedents

   A. The blessing of Jacob illustrates that the laying on of hands was an accepted practice in the earliest records of God's people.

Israel [Jacob] saw Joseph's sons, and said, "Who are these?"

Joseph said to his father, "They are my sons, whom God has given me in this place."

And he said, "Please bring them to me, and I will bless them." Now the eyes of Israel were dim with age, so that he could not see. Then Joseph brought them near him, and he kissed them and embraced them. And Israel said to Joseph, "I had not thought to see your face; but in fact, God has also shown me your offspring!"

So Joseph brought them from beside his knees, and he bowed down with his face to the earth. And Joseph took them both, Ephraim with his right hand toward Israel's left hand, and Manasseh with his left hand toward Israel's right hand, and brought them near him. Then Israel stretched out his right hand and laid it on Ephraim's head, who was the younger, and his left hand on Manasseh's head, guiding his hands knowingly, for Manasseh was the firstborn.

Genesis 48:8–14

Jacob (Israel) followed through with blessings that matched the purposeful placement of his hands. In spite of Joseph's fatherly positioning of his boys in the culturally expected positions—eldest son to be blessed by the right hand, which was understood to carry a higher blessing, and the younger son on the left hand—Jacob crossed his hands one over the other. He put his right hand on the younger son Ephraim's head and his left hand on the older son Manasseh's head.

By crossing his hands, Jacob released a spiritual, generational blessing to them in proportion to the positioning of his hands, not according to the boys' actual birth order. His blessing was borne out in its specifics over the subsequent generations. Jacob's laying on of hands carried great authority and power.

B. The lineage and legacy of Moses carries a strong element of the laying on of hands, as Joshua was appointed to be Moses' successor.

1. As Moses came near to the end of his life, he asked the Lord to appoint a new leader in his place.

The LORD said to Moses, "Take Joshua son of Nun, a man in whom is the spirit, and lay your hand on him. Have him stand before Eleazar the priest and the entire assembly and commission him in their presence. Give him some of your authority so the whole Israelite community will obey him."

Numbers 27:18–20, NIV

2. Moses followed God's instructions:

Moses did as the LORD commanded him. He took Joshua and had him stand before Eleazar the priest and the whole assembly.

Then he laid his hands on him and commissioned him, as the LORD instructed through Moses.

Numbers 27:22–23, NIV

3. As the result of this simple commissioning, authority and wisdom were imparted to Joshua, and the people respected him as their new leader:

> Joshua the son of Nun was full of the spirit of wisdom, for Moses had laid his hands on him; so the children of Israel heeded him, and did as the LORD had commanded Moses.

Deuteronomy 34:9

C. Elisha's deathbed prophetic act also demonstrates the power that can be transmitted through the laying on of hands. The king of Israel came to him with an urgent need, acknowledging by his greeting that Elisha's word held great power of Israel's military victories.

> Elisha had become sick with the illness of which he would die. Then Joash the king of Israel came down to him, and wept over his face, and said, "O my father, my father, the chariots of Israel and their horsemen!"
>
> And Elisha said to him, "Take a bow and some arrows." So he took himself a bow and some arrows. Then he said to the king of Israel, "Put your hand on the bow." So he put his hand on it, and Elisha put his hands on the king's hands. And he said, "Open the east window"; and he opened it. Then Elisha said, "Shoot"; and he shot. And he said, "The arrow of the LORD's deliverance and the arrow of deliverance from Syria; for you must strike the Syrians at Aphek till you have destroyed them."

2 Kings 13:14–17

Elisha, sick and infirm, did not shoot the arrow himself. He only put his hands on the king's hands and told him what to do, indicating by this prophetic gesture that God wanted the king to engage the Aramean enemy at Aphek. As it turned out, the king fell short in his follow-through, for which he was rebuked immediately by Elisha. His lukewarm response yielded only a partial victory on the battlefield. If he had taken advantage of the impartation of God's victorious strength through Elisha's hands and words, he could have prevailed.

This demonstrates not only the importance of the laying on of hands to impart strength, but also the value of receiving the full impartation and obeying any directives that God may choose to provide.

III. Impartation of the Holy Spirit's Gifts and Power

A. The laying on of hands enables the receiving of the Holy Spirit, becoming the "bridge" over which the impartation of His gifts and power often flows. For example, when the Church-persecutor Saul was struck down on the road to Damascus, his transformation was finalized through the visit of Ananias, who laid his hands on him and prophesied over him:

> Ananias went his way and entered the house; and *laying his hands on him* he said, "Brother Saul, the Lord Jesus, who appeared to you on the road as you came, has sent me that you may receive your sight and be filled with the Holy Spirit."
>
> Acts 9:17, emphasis added

Later, when Saul (by then called Paul) visited Ephesus and found twelve believers who had never even heard of the Holy Spirit, they received the Spirit and His gifts through the laying on of Paul's hands:

> Then Paul said, "John indeed baptized with a baptism of repentance, saying to the people that they should believe on Him who would come after him, that is, on Christ Jesus."
>
> When they heard this, they were baptized in the name of the Lord Jesus. And when Paul had *laid hands on them,* the Holy Spirit came upon them, and they spoke with tongues and prophesied.
>
> Acts 19:4–6, emphasis added

B. Paul desired to impart God's strength to believers everywhere, and he often employed the simple gesture of laying his hands on them. He wrote to the Roman believers:

> I am yearning to see you, that I may impart and share with you some spiritual gift to strengthen and establish you; that is, that we may be mutually strengthened and encouraged and comforted by each other's faith, both yours and mine.
>
> Romans 1:11–12, AMP

C. When the young disciple Timothy was commissioned by a group of prophets to serve the growing Church, we know they laid hands on him (see 1 Timothy 1:18 and 4:14).

D. The laying on of hands should be undertaken with these four wise safeguards:

1. This ministry should never be exercised lightly or carelessly, but always in a spirit of humility and prayer.
2. The Holy Spirit's guidance should be sought at every stage: with whom to pray, when to pray, how to pray.
3. The believer who lays hands on another must know how to claim on behalf of his own spirit the continual purifying and protecting power of the blood of Christ.
4. Believers who lay hands on others must themselves be so empowered by the Holy Spirit that they can overcome any kind of evil spiritual influence that may seek to work in or through the one upon whom hands have been laid.

IV. Ministering Compassion, Deliverance and Blessing

A. Jesus went about doing miracles of healing, frequently using the touch of His hands to heal even the "impossible" cases.

   1. Jesus set a pattern for the laying on of hands as a channel of healing:

> Departing from the region of Tyre and Sidon, He came through the midst of the region of Decapolis to the Sea of Galilee. Then they brought to Him one who was deaf and had an impediment in his speech, and they begged Him to put His hand on him. . . . Immediately his ears were opened, and the impediment of his tongue was loosed, and he spoke plainly.
>
> Mark 7:31–32, 35

> He took the blind man by the hand and led him out of the town. And when He had spit on his eyes and put His hands on him, He asked him if he saw anything.

> And he looked up and said, "I see men like trees, walking." Then He put His hands on his eyes again and made him look up. And he was restored and saw everyone clearly.
>
> Mark 8:23–25

> One of the rulers of the synagogue came, Jairus by name. And when he saw Him, he fell at His feet and begged Him earnestly, saying, "My little daughter lies at the point of death. Come and lay Your hands on her, that she may be healed, and she will live."
>
> Mark 5:22–23

   2. Jesus healed all who came to Him.

> When the sun was setting, all those who had any that were sick with various diseases brought them to Him; and He laid His hands on every one of them and healed them.
>
> Luke 4:40

   3. Jesus said signs of healing would follow His disciples when they would lay hands on the sick.

> These signs will follow those who believe: In My name they will cast out demons; they will speak with new tongues; they will take up serpents; and if they drink anything deadly, it will by no means hurt them; they will lay hands on the sick, and they will recover.
>
> Mark 16:17–18

   4. Elders of the early churches were instructed to anoint the sick with oil and to pray for them:

> Is anyone among you sick? Let him call for the elders of the church, and let them pray over him, anointing him with oil in the name of the Lord. And the prayer of faith will save the sick,

and the Lord will raise him up. And if he has committed sins, he will be forgiven.

James 5:14–15

B. In everything He does, the Holy Spirit ministers His very nature, which is love. Besides healing, His powerful touch causes the expelling of evil spirits (deliverance).

1. Paul was used by God in extraordinary miracles, including deliverance:

God worked unusual miracles by the hands of Paul, so that even handkerchiefs or aprons were brought from his body to the sick, and the diseases left them and the evil spirits went out of them.

Acts 19:11–12

2. As Jesus healed people, demons often left them: "Demons also came out of many, crying out and saying, 'You are the Christ, the Son of God!'" (Luke 4:41).

C. Jesus also modeled the laying on of hands for blessing. At first, the disciples did not appreciate the importance of this:

Some children were brought to Him so that He might lay His hands on them and pray; and the disciples rebuked them.

But Jesus said, "Let the children alone, and do not hinder them from coming to Me; for the kingdom of heaven belongs to such as these."

After laying His hands on them, He departed from there.

Matthew 19:13–15, NASB

V. Establishing Church Leadership

A. Through Church history, the laying on of hands has also been used to establish and consecrate men and women for roles of leadership in local churches as well as mobile church ministries.

1. The laying on of hands to establish local church ministries has included the consecration of deacons and elders.

a. The first deacons were set apart with prayer and the laying on of hands:

In those days, when the number of the disciples was multiplying, there arose a complaint against the Hebrews by the Hellenists, because their widows were neglected in the daily distribution. Then the twelve summoned the multitude of the disciples and said, "It is not desirable that we should leave the word of God and serve tables. Therefore, brethren, seek out from among you seven men of good reputation, full of the Holy Spirit and wisdom, whom we may appoint over this business; but we will give ourselves continually to prayer and to the ministry of the word."

And the saying pleased the whole multitude. And they chose Stephen, a man full of faith and the Holy Spirit, and Philip,

Prochorus, Nicanor, Timon, Parmenas, and Nicolas, a proselyte from Antioch, whom they set before the apostles; and when they had prayed, they laid hands on them.

Acts 6:1–6

b. The far-flung churches of the Roman Empire, including those of Lystra, Iconium and Antioch (the Antioch in Pisidia), were beginning to set apart elders to shepherd their churches. (See, for example, the notes in Acts 14:23 and 1 Timothy 5:17–22 about the establishment of elders elsewhere.)

2. The laying on of hands to establish mobile church ministries began as the early Church spread outside of Jerusalem:

There were at Antioch, in the church that was there, prophets and teachers: Barnabas, and Simeon who was called Niger, and Lucius of Cyrene, and Manaen who had been brought up with Herod the tetrarch, and Saul. While they were ministering to the Lord and fasting, the Holy Spirit said, "Set apart for Me Barnabas and Saul for the work to which I have called them."

Then, when they had fasted and prayed and laid their hands on them, they sent them away. So, being sent out by the Holy Spirit, they went down to Seleucia and from there they sailed to Cyprus.

Acts 13:1–4, NASB

B. The equipping of those who have been consecrated to minister involves the offices and gifts of the Holy Spirit. From the following passage, we often speak of these as the "five-fold" ministry of the Spirit:

His gifts were [varied; He Himself appointed and gave men to us] some to be apostles (special messengers), some prophets (inspired preachers and expounders), some evangelists (preachers of the Gospel, traveling missionaries), some pastors (shepherds of His flock) and teachers.

His intention was the perfecting and the full equipping of the saints (His consecrated people), [that they should do] the work of ministering toward building up Christ's body (the church), [That it might develop] until we all attain oneness in the faith and in the comprehension of the [full and accurate] knowledge of the Son of God, that [we might arrive] at really mature manhood (the completeness of personality which is nothing less than the standard height of Christ's own perfection), the measure of the stature of the fullness of the Christ and the completeness found in Him.

Ephesians 4:11–13, AMP

1. Wisdom indicates that believers should follow certain basic guidelines that Paul laid out for Timothy:

Elders who do their work well should be respected and paid well, especially those who work hard at both preaching and teaching. For the Scripture says, "You must not muzzle an ox to keep it from eating as it treads out the grain." And in another place, "Those who work deserve their pay!"

Do not listen to an accusation against an elder unless it is confirmed by two or three witnesses. Those who sin should be reprimanded in front of the whole church; this will serve as a strong warning to others. I solemnly command you in the presence of God and Christ Jesus and the holy angels to obey these instructions without taking sides or showing favoritism to anyone.

Never be in a hurry about appointing a church leader. Do not share in the sins of others. Keep yourself pure.

1 Timothy 5:17–22, NLT

2. The laying on of hands is equally important to the prayerful impartation of spiritual gifts, the ministration of healing and deliverance from evil spirits and the release of blessing, not to mention the consecration and setting apart of both local and trans-local church ministries. Under the inspiration of the Holy Spirit, our hands can do His work. Our hands are His hands on the earth.

Reflection Questions

Lesson 10: With These Hands

(Answers to these questions can be found in the back of the study guide.)

1. Fill in the blank:

   In spite of His disciples' disapproval, Jesus blessed _____ by laying hands on them.

   With the laying on of hands, the early Church set aside Stephen, Philip, Prochorus, Nicanor, Timon, Parmenas and Nicolas as the first _____.

   "I remind you to stir up the gift of God which is in you through _____. For God has not given us a spirit of fear, but of _____ and of love and of a sound mind."

2. What are the purposes of the laying on of hands? List at least three:

   _____
   _____
   _____

3. List four "wise safeguards" for the practice of the laying on of hands. (See section III. D.)

   (1)_____
   _____
   (2)_____
   _____
   (3)_____
   _____
   (4)_____
   _____

4. Multiple choice: Choose the correct name from the list to fill in the blanks.

   (a) Joshua
   (b) Moses

(c) Joash

(d) Isaac

(e) Jacob

(f) Ananias

(g) Paul

Joseph brought his two sons to his father, _____, so that his father could release a generational blessing to them by the laying on of hands.

When he discovered a dozen disciples who had never even heard of the Holy Spirit, _____ laid his hands on them and prayed for them to receive the Spirit.

The Israelites followed _____ as their new leader after Moses imparted authority to him through the laying on of his hands.

By the laying on of his hands, Elisha imparted wisdom and authority for military victory to _____.

After his Damascus Road experience, Saul received the Holy Spirit as well as healing for his sight when _____ laid his hands on him and prayed.

5. True or False:

The laying on of hands did not take place until the time of Christ and the early Church. _____

The laying on of hands is among the great foundational doctrines of the Christian faith. _____

The laying on of hands is reserved for leaders who have been ordained to official capacities. _____

Personal Application Question

6. Explain why this statement is true: "The laying on of hands links heaven and earth." How have you seen this proven in your own experience?

LESSON 11

RESURRECTION OF THE DEAD

I. **"He rose again from the dead. . . ."**

A. The resurrection of Jesus Christ is the foundational truth of the Good News of the Kingdom. The resurrection of Jesus is the hinge of history past, present and future.

B. Believers who recite the Apostle's Creed state that Jesus Christ was "crucified, died, and was buried. He descended into hell; the third day he rose again from the dead."

C. In the Old and New Testaments, three major groupings of resurrections have been noted:

1. bodily resurrections

2. spiritual resurrections of believers

3. the future resurrection of all people for judgment and reward

D. Resurrection is inseparably linked with teachings on eternal judgment.

II. **Resurrections—Past, Present and Future**

A. Where in Scripture do we find stories about past bodily resurrections?

1. Examples in the Old Testament:

a. Isaac's story is a "type," foreshadowing Jesus' resurrection. Even though Isaac did not end up dying after all, his father Abraham firmly believed that God could have raised him from death on that altar of sacrifice:

By faith Abraham, when God tested him, offered Isaac as a sacrifice. He who had received the promises was about to sacrifice his one and only son, even though God had said to him, "It is through Isaac that your offspring will be reckoned." Abraham reasoned that God could raise the dead, and figuratively speaking, he did receive Isaac back from death.

Hebrews 11:17–19, NIV

b. Elijah performed a physical resurrection when he raised the widow's son from the dead:

He took him out of her arms and carried him to the upper room where he was staying, and laid him on his own bed. Then he cried out to the LORD and said, "O LORD my God, have You also brought tragedy on the widow with whom I lodge, by killing her son?" And he stretched himself out on the child three times, and cried out to the LORD and said, "O LORD my God, I pray, let this child's soul come back to him." Then the LORD heard the voice of Elijah; and the soul of the child came back to him, and he revived.

And Elijah took the child and brought him down from the upper room into the house, and gave him to his mother. And Elijah said, "See, your son lives!"

1 Kings 17:19–23

c. Elijah was taken up into heaven without dying a physical death. His apparently complete escape from death qualifies as another "type" of resurrection from the dead. (See 2 Kings 2:1, 11.)

d. Like his master Elijah, Elisha raised another boy from the dead:

When Elisha came into the house, there was the child, lying dead on his bed. He went in therefore, shut the door behind the two of them, and prayed to the LORD. And he went up and lay on the child, and put his mouth on his mouth, his eyes on his eyes, and his hands on his hands; and he stretched himself out on the child, and the flesh of the child became warm. He returned and walked back and forth in the house, and again went up and stretched himself out on him; then the child sneezed seven times, and the child opened his eyes.

2 Kings 4:32–35

e. Enoch, father of Methuselah, who was known primarily for his incredibly long life, is known for never having died at all. He simply disappeared. The biblical account reads like this: "Enoch walked with God; and he was not, for God took him" (Genesis 5:24).

f. Throughout the time of the Old Testament, other unrecorded resurrections must have taken place. We base our assumption on the wording of a verse in the book of Hebrews, which mentions women receiving back their dead by resurrection (see Hebrews 11:35). This could include only the two women whose boys were raised from the dead by Elijah and Elisha, but it seems likely that more resurrections took place.

2. Examples in the New Testament:

a. The story of Lazarus, the friend of Jesus (see John 11:44)

b. The raising of the synagogue ruler's recently deceased daughter (see Mark 5:41–42)

    c. The graveyard resurrections of saints at the moment of Jesus' death by crucifixion (see Matthew 27:50–54)

    d. The prophetic resurrection of the two witnesses in Revelation (see Revelation 11:1–13)

B. The bodily resurrection of Jesus Christ was an unprecedented, unequalled historical moment, accompanied by many signs of its eternal significance such as an earthquake, the ripping of the Temple curtain from top to bottom and the resurrection of dead saints who walked the streets. After His resurrection on Easter morning, nothing would ever be the same again. Each of the gospel accounts includes different details:

    1. After the Sabbath, as the first day of the week began to dawn, Mary Magdalene and the other Mary came to see the tomb. And behold, there was a great earthquake; for an angel of the Lord descended from heaven, and came and rolled back the stone from the door, and sat on it. His countenance was like lightning, and his clothing as white as snow. And the guards shook for fear of him, and became like dead men.

    But the angel answered and said to the women, "Do not be afraid, for I know that you seek Jesus who was crucified. He is not here; for He is risen, as He said. Come, see the place where the Lord lay. And go quickly and tell His disciples that He is risen from the dead, and indeed He is going before you into Galilee; there you will see Him. Behold, I have told you."

    So they went out quickly from the tomb with fear and great joy, and ran to bring His disciples word.

    And as they went to tell His disciples, behold, Jesus met them, saying, "Rejoice!" So they came and held Him by the feet and worshiped Him. Then Jesus said to them, "Do not be afraid. Go and tell My brethren to go to Galilee, and there they will see Me."

                                          Matthew 28:1–10

    2. Entering the tomb, they saw a young man clothed in a long white robe sitting on the right side; and they were alarmed. But he said to them, "Do not be alarmed. You seek Jesus of Nazareth, who was crucified. He is risen! He is not here. See the place where they laid Him. But go, tell His disciples—and Peter—that He is going before you into Galilee; there you will see Him, as He said to you." So they went out quickly and fled from the tomb, for they trembled and were amazed. And they said nothing to anyone, for they were afraid.

    Now when He rose early on the first day of the week, He appeared first to Mary Magdalene, out of whom He had cast seven demons. She went and told those who had been with Him, as they mourned and wept. And when they heard that He was alive and had been seen by her, they did not believe.

After that, He appeared in another form to two of them as they walked and went into the country. And they went and told it to the rest, but they did not believe them either.

Mark 16:5–13

3. On the first day of the week, very early in the morning, they, and certain other women with them, came to the tomb bringing the spices which they had prepared. But they found the stone rolled away from the tomb. Then they went in and did not find the body of the Lord Jesus. And it happened, as they were greatly perplexed about this, that behold, two men stood by them in shining garments. Then, as they were afraid and bowed their faces to the earth, they said to them, "Why do you seek the living among the dead? He is not here, but is risen! Remember how He spoke to you when He was still in Galilee, saying, 'The Son of Man must be delivered into the hands of sinful men, and be crucified, and the third day rise again.'"

Luke 24:1–7

4. The first day of the week Mary Magdalene went to the tomb early, while it was still dark, and saw that the stone had been taken away from the tomb. Then she ran and came to Simon Peter, and to the other disciple, whom Jesus loved, and said to them, "They have taken away the Lord out of the tomb, and we do not know where they have laid Him."

Peter therefore went out, and the other disciple, and were going to the tomb. So they both ran together, and the other disciple outran Peter and came to the tomb first. And he, stooping down and looking in, saw the linen cloths lying there; yet he did not go in. Then Simon Peter came, following him, and went into the tomb; and he saw the linen cloths lying there, and the handkerchief that had been around His head, not lying with the linen cloths, but folded together in a place by itself. Then the other disciple, who came to the tomb first, went in also; and he saw and believed. For as yet they did not know the Scripture, that He must rise again from the dead.

John 20:1–9

C. Each believer shares in the spiritual resurrection of Jesus. Through His death and resurrection, Jesus made Himself one with sinners so that we could share in His death, burial, resurrection and later ascension. This is the core of our faith.

Therefore, whether or not we fully realize it, we have already experienced a resurrection. In a spiritual sense, we have died to our old life and we have been raised to new life (see Romans 6:1–11).

1. You were buried with Christ when you were baptized. And with him you were raised to new life because you trusted the mighty power of God, who raised Christ from the dead.

Colossians 2:12, NLT

2. You He made alive, who were dead in trespasses and sins, in which you once walked according to the course of this world, according to the prince of the power of the air, the spirit who now works in the sons of disobedience, among whom also we all once conducted ourselves in the lusts of our flesh, fulfilling the desires of the flesh and of the mind, and were by nature children of wrath, just as the others.

But God, who is rich in mercy, because of His great love with which He loved us, even when we were dead in trespasses, made us alive together with Christ (by grace you have been saved), and raised us up together, and made us sit together in the heavenly places in Christ Jesus, that in the ages to come He might show the exceeding riches of His grace in His kindness toward us in Christ Jesus. For by grace you have been saved through faith, and that not of yourselves; it is the gift of God, not of works, lest anyone should boast. For we are His workmanship, created in Christ Jesus for good works, which God prepared beforehand that we should walk in them.

Ephesians 2:1–10

3. When I tried to keep the law, it condemned me. So I died to the law—I stopped trying to meet all its requirements—so that I might live for God. My old self has been crucified with Christ. It is no longer I who live, but Christ lives in me. So I live in this earthly body by trusting in the Son of God, who loved me and gave himself for me.

Galatians 2:19–20, NLT

4. The love of Christ controls us, having concluded this, that one died for all, therefore all died; and He died for all, so that they who live might no longer live for themselves, but for Him who died and rose again on their behalf. Therefore from now on we recognize no one according to the flesh; even though we have known Christ according to the flesh, yet now we know Him in this way no longer.

Therefore if anyone is in Christ, he is a new creature; the old things passed away; behold, new things have come.

2 Corinthians 5:14–17, NASB

5. Evidences of this spiritual resurrection include the following:
   a. Purity (see Romans 6:11)
   b. Newness of life (see Romans 6:4)
   c. A new master (see 2 Corinthians 5:15)
   d. A mind set on new things (see Colossians 3:1–2)

D. Throughout Church history, resurrections have continued to occur. Jesus clearly commissioned His disciples to "heal the sick, cleanse the lepers, *raise the dead,* cast out demons. Freely you have received, freely give" (Matthew 10:8, emphasis added). By the time Luke wrote the Acts of the Apostles, he reported that Paul told King Agrippa, "Why should it be thought incredible by you that God raises the dead?" (Acts 26:8).

Phenomenal resurrections did not end with the apostolic era, as so many people have claimed. Although the expectation level was highest in the early days of the life of the Church, such miracles continued wherever people of faith encountered the need.

E. Resurrections take place to the present day. I am personally aware of a number of resurrections from the dead that have taken place in many countries of the world, including Africa, Mexico, Cambodia, Haiti and the Czech Republic. My dear friend and healing evangelist Mahesh Chavda has prayed for more than one person who has been subsequently raised from the dead. Indigenous leaders who work with Rolland and Heidi Baker of Iris Ministries in Mozambique have recorded over thirty resurrections. The ministry of David Hogan in Mexico has tallied story after story of healings, miracles and resurrections from the dead.

F. All believers await their future resurrection. The Apostle's Creed ends with these words: "I believe in . . . the resurrection of the body, and life everlasting." Without understanding exactly what it will consist of, believers are sure that a day will come when their earthly bodies will be perfected and their spirits will be satiated with Life.

1. "He will send out his angels with the mighty blast of a trumpet, and they will gather his chosen ones from all over the world—from the farthest ends of the earth and heaven."

Matthew 24:31, NLT

2. "Truly, truly, I say to you, an hour is coming and now is, when the dead will hear the voice of the Son of God, and those who hear will live."

John 5:25, NASB

3. This is the will of God, that I should not lose even one of all those he has given me, but that I should raise them up at the last day. For it is my Father's will that all who see his Son and believe in him should have eternal life. I will raise them up at the last day.

John 6:39–40, NLT

G. Unbelievers will experience a future resurrection too—to judgment. According to the Bible, unbelievers most certainly will experience resurrection too at some point in time for the sake of judgment.

1. Jesus said,

Truly, truly, I say to you, he who hears My word, and believes Him who sent Me, has eternal life, and does not come into judgment, but has passed out of death into life.

Truly, truly, I say to you, an hour is coming and now is, when the dead will hear the voice of the Son of God, and those who hear will live. For just as the Father has life in Himself, even so He gave to the Son also to have life in Himself; and He gave Him authority to execute judgment, because He is the Son of Man.

Do not marvel at this; for an hour is coming, in which all who are in the tombs will hear His voice, and will come forth; those who did the good deeds to a resurrection of life, those who committed the evil deeds to a resurrection of judgment.

John 5:24–29, NASB

2. The Christian belief in the judgment of both righteous and wicked people comes from the Jewish belief. Paul, in his verbal defense before the governor, Felix, referred to his accusers, the Jews, and he said, "I have hope in God, which they themselves also accept, that there will be a resurrection of the dead, both of the just and the unjust" (Acts 24:15).

III. The Resurrection of Jesus Christ

A. The resurrection of Jesus is the hinge of all history, past, present and future because all other resurrections—indeed, life itself—turns on that one event, which forever wedded together the realms of heaven and earth.

1. Jesus' resurrection had been foretold in the Old Testament (see Psalm 16:10 and Psalm 71:20–21).

2. Jesus Himself had predicted it (see Matthew 16:21; Matthew 17:22–23).

3. Peter quoted Psalm 16:10 in his Pentecost sermon: "You will not abandon me to the grave, nor will you let your Holy One see decay" (Acts 2:27, NIV), showing his listeners that what had just happened to Jesus had been foreseen by David much earlier. He went on to cite other prophetic words from the Old Testament that had now found their fulfillment in Jesus (see Acts 2:30–31):

a. The LORD has sworn in truth to David;

He will not turn from it:
"I will set upon your throne the fruit of your body."

Psalm 132:11

b. When your days are fulfilled and you rest with your fathers, I will set up your seed after you, who will come from your body, and I will establish his kingdom.

2 Samuel 7:12

c. I have made a covenant with My chosen, I have sworn to My servant David: Your seed I will establish forever, and build up your throne to all generations.

Psalm 89:3–4

4. Before He was crucified, Jesus had stated clearly what was about to happen:

   a. From that time on Jesus began to explain to his disciples that he must go to Jerusalem and suffer many things at the hands of the elders, chief priests and teachers of the law, and that he must be killed and on the third day be raised to life.

Matthew 16:21, NIV

   b. When they came together in Galilee, he said to them, "The Son of Man is going to be betrayed into the hands of men. They will kill him, and on the third day he will be raised to life." And the disciples were filled with grief.

Matthew 17:22–23, NIV

5. Then, once it happened, other people—too many of them to deny the validity of what they had seen—saw Him alive. He had been resurrected, just as He had predicted! (See 1 Corinthians 15:5–6.)

6. From then on, the resurrection of Jesus Christ was central to the preaching of the Gospel message (see 1 Corinthians 15:3–4) and therefore essential to individual salvation: "If you confess with your mouth the Lord Jesus and believe in your heart that God has raised Him from the dead, you will be saved" (Romans 10:9).

B. What did the resurrection of Jesus Christ from the dead accomplish? In summary, the historical fact of the resurrection speaks of all the ramifications of Kingdom citizenship:

1. His resurrection designates Jesus as the Son of God (see Acts 2:32–33; Romans 1:4).

2. Through Jesus' resurrection, death was defeated (see Romans 6:9; Revelation 1:18).

3. Through Jesus' resurrection, believers obtain justification (see Romans 4:25).

4. Through Jesus' resurrection, believers obtain "newness of life" and sanctification (see Romans 6:4).

5. Now that death has been defeated, believers' bodies can be raised imperishable, in glory and in power (see 1 Corinthians 15:42–23).

6. Because of His resurrection, Jesus Christ reigns supreme (see Ephesians 1:20–23; Matthew 28:19).

7. Because of Jesus' resurrection, a Man is on the throne (see Hebrews 10:12).

8. Because of Jesus' resurrection, believers have a new hope (see 1 Peter 1:3).

9. Because of Jesus' resurrection, future judgment is assured (see Acts 17:31).

IV. The Ultimate Resurrection of All Who Are in the Grave

A. The Bible indicates that every human being who has ever lived will be resurrected.

1. Do not marvel at this; for an hour is coming, in which all who are in the tombs will hear His voice, and will come forth; those who did the good deeds to a resurrection of life, those who committed the evil deeds to a resurrection of judgment.

John 5:28–29, NASB

2. I tell you a mystery; we will not all sleep, but we will all be changed, in a moment, in the twinkling of an eye, at the last trumpet; for the trumpet will sound, and the dead will be raised imperishable, and we will be changed.

1 Corinthians 15:51–52, NASB

B. This last-day scenario seems impossible, given the decomposition of dead flesh over the course of history. It is possible because each dead person was, like each person who is alive right now, a triune being: spirit and soul housed in a body.

1. Note the divine order in Paul's listing of the three components of a complete human being:

May the God of peace Himself sanctify you completely; and may your whole spirit, soul, and body be preserved blameless at the coming of our Lord Jesus Christ.

1 Thessalonians 5:23

2. Made in the image of the triune God (see Genesis 1:26–27), each one of us is a three-part harmony. Soul and spirit differ from each other, although only God Himself can penetrate to their dividing place (see Hebrews 4:12).

3. The spirit and soul outlive death, returning to God, while the body returns to the dust from which it came. In other words, each part returns to its place of origin at the time of physical death: "Then the dust will return to the earth as it was, and the spirit will return to God who gave it" (Ecclesiastes 12:7).

C. What is the destination of the human spirit after death?

1. Until Christ's resurrection, all of the dead were confined in Sheol or Hades, which had two parts—one a place of comfort and rest, and the other a place of torment.

Sheol (Hades, the place of the dead) below is stirred up to meet you at your coming [O tyrant Babylonian rulers]; it stirs up the shades of the dead to greet you—even all the chief ones of the earth; it raises from their thrones [in astonishment at your humbled condition] all the kings of the nations. All of them will [tauntingly] say to you, Have you also become weak as we are? Have you become like us?

Isaiah 14:9–10, AMP

2. Luke tells us the story of Lazarus and the rich man (see Luke 16:19–31). Abraham, known to us as a father of the faith, was also in this temporary holding place called Hades, waiting for Jesus to come, descend into hell and lead captivity captive (see Ephesians 4:8; Colossians 2:15).

D. The "holding place" is history. Now when believers die, they are immediately present with the Lord. Our faith informs our expectations that our spirits will outlive our bodies. In this post-resurrection era of the New Testament covenant, we understand that when believers die, no longer must their spirits languish in a temporary waiting place.

1. Stephen, as he was being stoned to death, could see into heaven and knew that his spirit would be going there as soon as he died:

> Stephen, full of the Holy Spirit, looked up to heaven and saw the glory of God, and Jesus standing at the right hand of God. "Look," he said, "I see heaven open and the Son of Man standing at the right hand of God."
>
> . . . While they were stoning him, Stephen prayed, "Lord Jesus, receive my spirit."
>
> Acts 7:55–56, 59, NIV

2. Like Stephen, we too assume that after death, our spirits will depart from this world and be ushered into the presence of God.

> We are always confident, even though we know that as long as we live in these bodies we are not at home with the Lord. For we live by believing and not by seeing. Yes, we are fully confident, and we would rather be away from these earthly bodies, for then we will be at home with the Lord. So whether we are here in this body or away from this body, our goal is to please him.
>
> 2 Corinthians 5:6–9, NLT (see also Philippians 1:21–24)

E. God has a precise record of our earthly bodies, down to the last hair:

> The very hairs of your head are all numbered.
>
> Matthew 10:30, AMP

> You will be hated by all for My name's sake. But not a hair of your head shall be lost.
>
> Luke 21:17–18

F. In the last day when that heavenly trumpet sounds, the supernatural power of the wind of God will reconstruct and bring together the three essential parts of every person: spirits, souls and even the "dust" of the body that has been dispersed across the face of the earth and has disappeared into the elements.

The material, earthly elements of which we are composed were appointed and prepared beforehand by God for the making of our bodies. (See Psalm 139:13–16, for example.) And He keeps track of everything in His universe.

1. "We will not all sleep, but we will all be changed" (1 Corinthians 15:51, NASB). Faster than the time it took you to read this sentence, we will all be reassembled in perfect and glorified bodies. Physically. That is what resurrection is about:

> "Look at my hands and my feet. It is I myself! Touch me and see; a ghost does not have flesh and bones, as you see I have." When he had said this, he showed them his hands and feet.
>
> Luke 24:39–40, NIV (see also John 20:27)

2. Jesus reiterated,

> Most assuredly, I say to you, the hour is coming, and now is, when the dead will hear the voice of the Son of God; and those who hear will live. . . . Do not marvel at this; for the hour is coming in which all who are in the graves will hear His voice and come forth—those who have done good, to the resurrection of life, and those who have done evil, to the resurrection of condemnation.
>
> John 5:25, 28–29

G. Jesus Christ is the "firstfruits of those who have fallen asleep [who have died]" (1 Corinthians 15:20). Furthermore,

> Since [it was] through a man that death [came into the world, it is] also through a Man that the resurrection of the dead [has come]. For just as [because of their union of nature] in Adam all people die, so also [by virtue of their union of nature] shall all in Christ be made alive.
>
> But each in his own rank and turn: Christ (the Messiah) [is] the firstfruits, then those who are Christ's [own will be resurrected] at His coming. After that comes the end (the completion), when He delivers over the kingdom to God the Father after rendering inoperative and abolishing every [other] rule and every authority and power.
>
> 1 Corinthians 15:21–24, AMP

1. God's purpose is to take everything back, tossing out anything that is impure and restoring everything to the glory of its first creation.

2. We are His own children, His heirs and co-heirs with our eldest Brother, Jesus, "if indeed we share in his sufferings in order that we may also share in his glory. . . . Our present sufferings are not worth comparing with the glory that will be revealed in us" (Romans 8:17–18, NIV).

V. The Resurrection—the Hinge of History

    A. Through Jesus' resurrection we have access not only to eternal life with Him, but also to abundance here and now, including the following:

        1. Personal holiness (see Titus 2:11–14; 1 John 3:3).

        2. Personal encouragement, hope and comfort (see 1 Thessalonians 4:13–18; 1 Thessalonians 5:9–11; 1 Peter 1:3).

        3. Balance in our Christian lives (see Matthew 24:45–51; Matthew 25:1–13).

        4. Motivation to persevere (see Romans 8:17–18).

        5. Resurrection power (see Romans 1:4; Ephesians 1:17–20; Philippians 3:10).

    B. "If the Spirit of Him who raised Jesus from the dead dwells in you, He who raised Christ from the dead will also give life to your mortal bodies through His Spirit who dwells in you" (Romans 8:11).

Reflection Questions

Lesson 11: Resurrection of the Dead

(Answers to these questions can be found in the back of the study guide.)

1. True or false:

   The resurrection of Jesus Christ was foretold in the Old Testament. _____

   At the time of the resurrection, God will do away completely with our former physical bodies. _____

   Unbelieving sinners will be resurrected, too. _____

2. Fill in the blank:

   The resurrection of Jesus Christ is the _____ of all history, past, present and future.

   If the Spirit of Him who raised Jesus from the dead dwells in you, He who raised Christ from the dead will also give _____ to your mortal bodies through His Spirit who dwells in you.

   An hour is coming, in which all who are in the tombs will hear His voice, and will come forth; those who did the good deeds to a resurrection of _____, those who committed the evil deeds to a resurrection of _____.

3. Human beings are triune just as their Creator is. List a person's three components, *in order of importance:*

   a. _____
   b. _____
   c. _____

4. Multiple choice: Choose the best answer from the list.
   (a) Satan
   (b) miracle-working power
   (c) ungodliness
   (d) resurrection

   The _____ of Jesus Christ is foundational to the Good News of the Kingdom.

The grace of God brings salvation to everyone, instructing us to deny _____, to live godly lives and to look for the appearing of Christ.

5. What nine things did the resurrection of Jesus Christ accomplish? (Refer to section III. B.)

(1)_____

_____

(2)_____

_____

(3)_____

_____

(4)_____

_____

(5)_____

_____

(6)_____

_____

(7)_____

_____

(8)_____

_____

(9)_____

_____

Personal Application Question

6. How has this lesson expanded your understanding of the resurrection from the dead?

LESSON 12

ETERNAL JUDGMENT

I. Eternal Judgment vs. Historical Judgment

A. *Judgment* itself is a neutral word; it can indicate both negative punishments and positive rewards.

B. Historical judgments, as summed up in Exodus 20:5–6 and Jeremiah 32:18, occur as the result of far-reaching curses that may or may not reflect on the merit of the individuals affected by them.

1. I, the LORD your God, am a jealous God, visiting the iniquity of the fathers upon the children to the third and fourth generations of those who hate Me, but showing mercy to thousands, to those who love Me and keep My commandments.

   Exodus 20:5–6

2. You show lovingkindness to thousands, and repay the iniquity of the fathers into the bosom of their children after them—the Great, the Mighty God, whose name is the LORD of hosts.

   Jeremiah 32:18

C. God's eternal judgment does reflect on each individual person; each person will stand alone before Him in the end. No one can ride on the coattails of another person, nor can the sin of another consign you to condemnation. This truth goes back to the Old Testament:

> The word of the LORD came to me again, saying, "What do you mean when you use this proverb concerning the land of Israel, saying:
>
> > 'The fathers have eaten sour grapes,
> > And the children's teeth are set on edge'?
>
> "As I live," says the Lord GOD, "you shall no longer use this proverb in Israel.

"Behold, all souls are Mine; the soul of the father as well as the soul of the son is Mine; the soul who sins shall die. . . .

"The soul who sins shall die. The son shall not bear the guilt of the father, nor the father bear the guilt of the son. The righteousness of the righteous shall be upon himself, and the wickedness of the wicked shall be upon himself. . . .

"But when a righteous man turns away from his righteousness and commits iniquity, and does according to all the abominations that the wicked man does, shall he live? All the righteousness which he has done shall not be remembered; because of the unfaithfulness of which he is guilty and the sin which he has committed, because of them he shall die."

Ezekiel 18:1–4, 20, 24

II. The Protocol of God's Judgments

A. Because God the Father will judge us, we need to both establish our lives on the firm foundation of His truth and conduct ourselves according to our faith.

1. Peter's advice to the early Church applies to us today: "Since you call on a Father who judges each man's work impartially, live your lives as strangers here in reverent fear" (1 Peter 1:17, NIV).

2. We are living in the last days, heading toward the end times—and Judgment Day. Looking forward, we cannot shrug off warnings about unrighteousness as we redouble our efforts to trust wholeheartedly in our Savior Jesus:

You have come to Mount Zion and to the city of the living God, the heavenly Jerusalem, to an innumerable company of angels, to the general assembly and church of the firstborn who are registered in heaven, to God the Judge of all, to the spirits of just men made perfect, to Jesus the Mediator of the new covenant, and to the blood of sprinkling that speaks better things than that of Abel. . . .

Therefore, since we are receiving a kingdom which cannot be shaken, let us have grace, by which we may serve God acceptably with reverence and godly fear. For our God is a consuming fire.

Hebrews 12:22–24, 28–29

B. The Father is the Judge, but He has entrusted the duty of judging to His Son, who is also our Savior. Jesus knows His own, and He can see every nuance of a person's actions. Did this one build in the flesh, or in the Spirit? To build, what did this person choose to use—hay and stubble, or gold and silver?

1. The Father judges no one, but has committed all judgment to the Son, that all should honor the Son just as they honor the Father. He who does not honor the Son does not honor the Father who sent Him. . . . For as the Father has life in Himself,

so He has granted the Son to have life in Himself, and has given Him authority to execute judgment also, because He is the Son of Man.

John 5:22–23, 26–27

2. He [Jesus] commanded us to preach to the people, and to testify that it is He who was ordained by God to be Judge of the living and the dead.

Acts 10:42

C. The Father "has given him authority to judge because he is the Son of Man" (John 5:27, NIV). The Son of Man is also the Living Word, and He has told us that His words, which are eternal, will be sufficient to judge a person:

1. If anyone hears My words and does not believe, I do not judge him; for I did not come to judge the world but to save the world. He who rejects Me, and does not receive My words, has that which judges him—the word that I have spoken will judge him in the last day.

John 12:47–48

2. The entirety of Your word is truth,

> And every one of Your righteous judgments endures
> forever.

Psalm 119:160

D. The protocol of eternal judgment can be summed up according to four main principles:

1. According to truth (see Romans 2:1–2)
2. According to deeds (see Romans 2:6)
3. Without partiality (see Romans 2:11)
4. According to the light available to those being judged (see Romans 2:12)

III. The Judgment Seat of Christ for All Believers

A. Each person (beginning with believers) will stand before the judgment seat of Christ.

1. We shall all stand before the judgment seat of Christ. For it is written:

> "As I live, says the LORD,
> Every knee shall bow to Me,
> And every tongue shall confess to God."

So then each of us shall give account of himself to God.

Romans 14:10–12

2. The time has come for judgment to begin at the house of God; and if it begins with us first, what will be the end of those who do not obey the gospel of God? Now

> "If the righteous one is scarcely saved,
> Where will the ungodly and the sinner appear?"
>
> 1 Peter 4:17–18

3. We must all appear before the judgment seat of Christ, that each one may receive the things done in the body, according to what he has done, whether good or bad.

2 Corinthians 5:10

B. Those who have put their trust in Christ Jesus should not be afraid about standing before His judgment seat, because He will mete out *rewards,* not condemnation, purifying you of your transgressions.

1. I assure you, most solemnly I tell you, the person whose ears are open to My words [who listens to My message] and believes and trusts in and clings to and relies on Him Who sent Me has (possesses now) eternal life. And he does not come into judgment [does not incur sentence of judgment, will not come under condemnation], but he has already passed over out of death into life.

John 5:24, AMP

2. I, even I, am he who blots out

> your transgressions, for my own sake,
> and remembers your sins no more. . . .
> I have swept away your offenses like a cloud,
> your sins like the morning mist.
> Return to me,
> for I have redeemed you.

Isaiah 43:25; 44:22, NIV

3. I tell you this, you must give an account on judgment day for every idle word you speak. The words you say will either acquit you or condemn you.

Matthew 12:36–37, NLT

4. John, Jesus' beloved disciple, reassured believers that only their unbelief would be relegated to condemnation, when he wrote that "he who believes in Him is not condemned; but he who does not believe is condemned already, because he has not believed in the name of the only begotten Son of God" (John 3:18).

5. The Son of Man will come with his angels in the glory of his Father and will judge all people according to their deeds.

Matthew 16:27, NLT

6. Since we have now been justified by his blood, how much more shall we be saved from God's wrath through him! For

if, when we were God's enemies, we were reconciled to him through the death of his Son, how much more, having been reconciled, shall we be saved through his life! . . .

Therefore, there is now no condemnation for those who are in Christ Jesus.

Romans 5:9–10; 8:1 NIV

C. All of our good works will be tried by fire and only the pure will remain.

1. Because of God's grace to me, I have laid the foundation like an expert builder. Now others are building on it. But whoever is building on this foundation must be very careful. For no one can lay any foundation other than the one we already have—Jesus Christ.

Anyone who builds on that foundation may use a variety of materials—gold, silver, jewels, wood, hay, or straw. But on the judgment day, fire will reveal what kind of work each builder has done. The fire will show if a person's work has any value. If the work survives, that builder will receive a reward. But if the work is burned up, the builder will suffer great loss. The builder will be saved, but like someone barely escaping through a wall of flames.

Don't you realize that all of you together are the temple of God and that the Spirit of God lives in you?

1 Corinthians 3:10–16, NLT

2. The entire parable of the talents, which is where we hear "Well done, good and faithful servant," exposes this same view of God's judgment (see Matthew 25:14–30; Luke 19:11–27).

3. Our goal should be to keep a clear conscience on every level, remembering that today's actions determine tomorrow's rewards—all the while trusting ourselves to the One who will judge us in the end (see 1 Corinthians 4:5).

D. Each of us should examine ourselves on the following three points:

1. We should examine our motives. Do we seek to glorify Jesus Christ or do we aim to please ourselves?

2. We should examine ourselves on the point of obedience. Are we performing God's will or doing our own thing?

3. We should examine ourselves with respect to power. Are we serving God in our own strength or in His power?

   a. "The kingdom of God is not in word but in power" (1 Corinthians 4:20).

   b. "To this end I labor, struggling with all his energy, which so powerfully works in me" (Colossians 1:29, NIV).

IV. Judgment of the Nations

A. I believe that many times of tribulations have and will occur upon the earth, but that only one final period of time qualifies as the

Great Tribulation, and that at the close of the Great Tribulation, a period of seven years, the nations of the earth will face the judgment of God.

Those nations that are deemed worthy, having passed through the refining fires of the Great Tribulation, will enter into a thousand years of peace, also known as the millennial Kingdom, which Jesus Christ will establish on the earth. These nations will continue on as geographical entities, places of rule and dominion, while Satan will be chained in the "bottomless pit" and martyrs will be raised from the dead in what is known as the "first resurrection," to help rule the nations. Later, Satan will be released for a short time, but not until the thousand years is finished. (For background on all of this, see the first six verses of chapter 20 in the apostle John's book of Revelation.)

Here is what Jesus told us about this time of judgment:

When the Son of Man comes in His glory, and all the holy angels with Him, then He will sit on the throne of His glory. All the nations will be gathered before Him, and He will separate them one from another, as a shepherd divides his sheep from the goats. And He will set the sheep on His right hand, but the goats on the left. Then the King will say to those on His right hand, "Come, you blessed of My Father, inherit the kingdom prepared for you from the foundation of the world: for I was hungry and you gave Me food; I was thirsty and you gave Me drink; I was a stranger and you took Me in; I was naked and you clothed Me; I was sick and you visited Me; I was in prison and you came to Me."

Then the righteous will answer Him, saying, "Lord, when did we see You hungry and feed You, or thirsty and give You drink? When did we see You a stranger and take You in, or naked and clothe You? Or when did we see You sick, or in prison, and come to You?" And the King will answer and say to them, "Assuredly, I say to you, inasmuch as you did it to one of the least of these My brethren, you did it to Me."

Then He will also say to those on the left hand, "Depart from Me, you cursed, into the everlasting fire prepared for the devil and his angels: for I was hungry and you gave Me no food; I was thirsty and you gave Me no drink; I was a stranger and you did not take Me in, naked and you did not clothe Me, sick and in prison and you did not visit Me."

Then they also will answer Him, saying, "Lord, when did we see You hungry or thirsty or a stranger or naked or sick or in prison, and did not minister to You?" Then He will answer them, saying, "Assuredly, I say to you, inasmuch as you did not do it to one of the least of these, you did not do it to Me." And these will go away into everlasting punishment, but the righteous into eternal life.

Matthew 25:31–46

B. First, God will regather the scattered Jewish people to their own land, then He will gather all the Gentile nations and bring final judgment upon them. The basis of this judgment is the same as that described by Jesus in Matthew 25. Through the prophet Joel, God says He will enter into judgment with the nations "on account of My people Israel":

> Behold, in those days and at that time,
> When I bring back the captives of Judah and Jerusalem,
> I will also gather all nations,
> And bring them down to the Valley of Jehoshaphat;
> And I will enter into judgment with them there
> On account of My people, My heritage Israel,
> Whom they have scattered among the nations;
> They have also divided up My land.
>
> Joel 3:1–2

V. Special Judgment upon Israel

A. For more than sixty years, the Jewish people have again had a homeland. Soon, however, according to Jeremiah 30:3–9, they will enter into a time of both consolidation and national distress more terrible than any previous time. All of this is leading up to a great denouement, when the Lord Himself will intervene against the Gentile enemies of Israel. He will deliver and save Israel, and the national kingdom of Israel will again be restored upon the throne of David, under the supreme government of the Lord Jesus Christ Himself. This period of the restored kingdom is called the Millennium.

1. "Behold, the days are coming," says the LORD, "that I will bring back from captivity My people Israel and Judah," says the LORD. "And I will cause them to return to the land that I gave to their fathers, and they shall possess it."

   Now these are the words that the LORD spoke concerning Israel and Judah.

   "For thus says the LORD:

   > 'We have heard a voice of trembling,
   > Of fear, and not of peace.
   > Ask now, and see,
   > Whether a man is ever in labor with child?
   > So why do I see every man with his hands on his loins
   > Like a woman in labor,
   > And all faces turned pale?
   > Alas! For that day is great,
   > So that none is like it;
   > And it is the time of Jacob's trouble,
   > But he shall be saved out of it.
   > For it shall come to pass in that day,'
   > Says the LORD of hosts,

'That I will break his yoke from your neck,
And will burst your bonds;
Foreigners shall no more enslave them.
But they shall serve the LORD their God,
And David their king,
Whom I will raise up for them.'"

Jeremiah 30:3–9

2. This period of the restored kingdom is called the Millennium. But first, the Gentiles, as God's instrument of judgment, will be stirred up against the Jews (see Zechariah 12:1–3; 14:1–4).

3. The Jewish nation will be purged clean as all rebellious elements are confronted and destroyed. Ultimately, what remains of Israel will turn to Christ, the One whom they have pierced (see Zechariah 12:10).

4. This reconciliation of the nation of Israel to their Lord is described in the epistle to the Romans:

I want you to understand this mystery, dear brothers and sisters, so that you will not feel proud about yourselves. Some of the people of Israel have hard hearts, but this will last only until the full number of Gentiles comes to Christ. And so all Israel will be saved. As the Scriptures say,

"The one who rescues will come from Jerusalem,
and he will turn Israel away from ungodliness.
And this is my covenant with them,
that I will take away their sins."

Romans 11:25–27, NLT

B. At the end of the age, the Jewish nation will enter their own time of Great Tribulation. In this "time of Jacob's distress," they will cry out for the intervention of their Messiah—and Yeshua will come, bringing in the close of the Millennium.

1. Whereas God has normally blessed the Gentiles through the Jews, here He will bless the Jews directly.

2. And whereas God has normally punished the Jews through the Gentiles, now He will punish the Gentiles directly.

VI. The Great White Throne Judgment

A. After the close of the Millennium, Satan will be released from the bottomless pit for a time.

1. He will attempt to organize the Gentile nations to rebel against the Kingdom of Jesus Christ, but they will be destroyed. (See Revelation 20:3, 7–10.)

   In the destruction, the devil himself will be thrown into the "lake of fire and brimstone" (Revelation 20:10) along with other major adversaries in this epic battle.

2. Once Satan's last rebellion has been defeated, all the rebellion on the earth will have been purged. It will be time for all of the

dead who have not previously been judged to be resurrected and called forth to stand before what John saw as the great white throne. This is the second resurrection, and the final judgment. The second resurrection is different from the first resurrection spoken of in Revelation 20:4–6. None of those who rose in the first resurrection will die or need to be judged again.

Here is John's account:

I saw a great white throne and Him who sat on it, from whose face the earth and the heaven fled away. And there was found no place for them. And I saw the dead, small and great, standing before God, and books were opened. And another book was opened, which is the Book of Life. And the dead were judged according to their works, by the things which were written in the books. The sea gave up the dead who were in it, and Death and Hades delivered up the dead who were in them. And they were judged, each one according to his works. Then Death and Hades were cast into the lake of fire. This is the second death. And anyone not found written in the Book of Life was cast into the lake of fire. . . .

He who overcomes shall inherit all things, and I will be his God and he shall be My son. But the cowardly, unbelieving, abominable, murderers, sexually immoral, sorcerers, idolaters, and all liars shall have their part in the lake which burns with fire and brimstone, which is the second death.

Revelation 20:11–15; 21:7–8

B. Those whose names are written in the Book of Life will enter into the new earth, and those whose names do not appear will enter into the lake of fire where the rest of the wicked have gone. The splendor of heaven will descend to earth:

I saw a new heaven and a new earth, for the first heaven and the first earth had passed away. Also there was no more sea. Then I, John, saw the holy city, New Jerusalem, coming down out of heaven from God, prepared as a bride adorned for her husband. And I heard a loud voice from heaven saying, "Behold, the tabernacle of God is with men, and He will dwell with them, and they shall be His people. God Himself will be with them and be their God. And God will wipe away every tear from their eyes; there shall be no more death, nor sorrow, nor crying. There shall be no more pain, for the former things have passed away."

Then He who sat on the throne said, "Behold, I make all things new." And He said to me, "Write, for these words are true and faithful."

And He said to me, "It is done! I am the Alpha and the Omega, the Beginning and the End. I will give of the fountain of the water of life freely to him who thirsts."

Revelation 21:1–6, see also Revelation 22:12–13, 16–17

C. Those who have built their lives upon the firm foundation supplied by Jesus Christ will be privileged to be among the chosen ones, who, having kept their robes clean, cry out even now, "Come, Lord Jesus!" Jesus proclaims to His Bride, the Church:

> "Behold, I am coming soon! My reward is with me, and I will give to everyone according to what he has done. I am the Alpha and the Omega, the First and the Last, the Beginning and the End.

> "Blessed are those who wash their robes, that they may have the right to the tree of life and may go through the gates into the city. Outside are the dogs, those who practice magic arts, the sexually immoral, the murderers, the idolaters and everyone who loves and practices falsehood."

> The Spirit and the bride say, "Come!" And let him who hears say, "Come!" Whoever is thirsty, let him come; and whoever wishes, let him take the free gift of the water of life. . . .

> He who testifies to these things says, "Yes, I am coming soon."

> Amen. Come, Lord Jesus.

> The grace of the Lord Jesus be with God's people. Amen.

> Revelation 22:12–15, 17, 20–21, NIV

Reflection Questions

Lesson 12: Eternal Judgment

(Answers to these questions can be found in the back of the study guide.)

1. True or false:

   God will judge the Gentile nations based on their treatment of Israel.

   _____

   Each person will be individually judged in eternity for his or her own life. _____

   The national kingdom of Israel will again be restored under the supreme government of the Lord Jesus Christ Himself. _____

2. The "protocol" of God's eternal judgment can be summed up according to four main principles. List them below. (See section II. D.)

   (1)_____

   (2)_____

   (3)_____

   (4)_____

3. Fill in the blanks:

   "We shall all stand before the _____ seat of Christ.

      For it is written:

   "As I live, says the Lord,

   Every _____ shall bow to Me,

   And every _____ shall confess to God."

   So then each of us shall give account of himself to God.

   Romans 14:10–12

4. Multiple choice: Choose the best answers from the list.

   (a) fire

   (b) judgment

   (c) earth

   (c) heaven

   All of our good works will be tried by _____ and only the pure will remain.

Those whose names are written in the Book of Life will enter into the new _____, and those whose names do not appear will enter into the lake of fire.

5. Question: Why can you as a believer approach Judgment Day with confidence?
   (a) Because Judgment Day is for unbelievers, not for believers
   (b) Because the Judge, Jesus, will reward you, not condemn you, while purifying you of your transgressions
   (c) Because Jesus' blood exempts you from judgment

Personal Application Question

6. As a final "foundation check," examine yourself on the following three points. (See section III. D.)
   a. Examine your motives. Do you seek to glorify Jesus Christ or do you aim to please yourself?
   b. Examine yourself on the point of obedience. Are you performing God's will or doing your own thing?
   c. Examine yourself with respect to power. Are you serving God in your own strength or in His power? (See 1 Corinthians 4:20 and Colossians 1:29.)

ANSWERS TO REFLECTION QUESTIONS

Lesson 1: The Foundation for All Believers

1. foundation, foundation
2. (1) Personal confrontation by Christ, (2) A direct, spiritual revelation of Christ, (3) A personal acknowledgment of Christ, (4) An open and personal confession of Christ.
3. (a) Jesus Christ
4. Rock, cornerstone
5. (c) Your own

Lesson 2: The Amazing Word of God

1. Verses 84, 90, 121, 122, 132
2. mirror
3. See section I. B. of study outline.
4. See sections I. C., II and III of study outline.
5. Jesus Christ

Lesson 3: God in Three Persons

1. Father, Son, Holy Spirit
2. (b) persons
3. (a) polytheism
4. False, False, True
5. Genesis

Lesson 4: God's Plan for Salvation

1. (c) blood
2. save sinners
3. True, False, False
4. (b) People owe something because of sin; they must pay for it by means of death.
5. our faith

Lesson 5: Repentance from Dead Works

1. foundation, gift, change
2. False, False, True
3. (d) repentance, (c) works
4. (1) Godly sorrow, (2) Self-examination, (3) Confession to God, (4) Public confession, (5) Forsaking of sin, (6) Reconciliation, (7) Restitution, (8) Good works
5. works

Lesson 6: Grace Defined

1. (c) tutor, (d) salvation
2. grace
3. True, False, True
4. (a) Humble yourself, (b) Stop working and believe, (c) Receive more of Christ
5. mercy, grace

Lesson 7: Transforming Faith

1. sight, waiting
2. (d) words, (c) potential
3. True, True
4. (1) Preaching of the Gospel, (2) The written Word, (3) Times of prayer, (4) A word of testimony or exhortation, (5) Dreams, visions and supernatural experiences, (6) Audible voice of God
5. good works, good works, good works

Lesson 8: Vital: Water Baptism

1. (b) repent, (c) circumcise, (a) immerse
2. (1) Jesus commanded it. (2) Jesus Himself received baptism, giving us an example to follow. (3) Baptism demonstrates a clear conscience toward God. (4) Baptism testifies to the death, burial and resurrection of the Lord Jesus Christ. (5) Baptism testifies to the defeat of Satan. (6) A baptism is a public confession of faith and fellowship. (7) Baptism enables us to walk in newness of life. (8) Baptism is a witness to the world, the Church, God and ourselves.
3. True, True
4. Father, Son, Holy Spirit
5. death, Buried

Lesson 9: The Glorious Baptism in the Holy Spirit

1. True, False, True
2. (1) He will stay forever. (2) He will dwell in believers. (3) He will teach believers all things. (4) He will bring the words of Jesus to remembrance. (5) He will bear witness of Jesus. (6) He will convict the world. (7) He will guide believers into all truth. (8) He will glorify Jesus. (9) He will give us power.
3. All are symbols of or metaphors for the Holy Spirit.
4. heart, spirit, heart, heart
5. (b) power, (a) fruit, (c) transformation

Lesson 10: With These Hands

1. children, deacons, the laying on of hands, power
2. prayerful impartation of spiritual gifts, the ministration of healing, deliverance from evil spirits, the release of blessing, the consecration and setting apart of leaders for church ministries
3. (1) This ministry should never be exercised lightly or carelessly, but always in a spirit of humility and prayer. (2) The Holy Spirit's guidance should be sought at every stage: with whom to pray, when to pray, how to pray. (3) The believer who lays hands on another must know how to claim on behalf of his own spirit the continual purifying and protecting power of the blood of Christ. (4) Believers who lay hands on others must themselves be so empowered by the Holy Spirit that they can overcome any kind of evil spiritual influence that may seek to work in or through the one upon whom hands have been laid.
4. (e) Jacob, (g) Paul, (a) Joshua, (c) Joash, (f) Ananias
5. False, True, False

Lesson 11: Resurrection of the Dead

1. True, False, True
2. hinge, life, life, judgment
3. (a) spirit, (b) soul, (c) body
4. (d) resurrection, (c) ungodliness
5. (1) His resurrection designates Jesus as the Son of God. (2) Through Jesus' resurrection, death was defeated. (3) Through Jesus' resurrection, believers obtain justification. (4) Through Jesus' resurrection, believers obtain "newness of life" and sanctification. (5) Now that death has been defeated, believers' bodies can be raised imperishable, in glory and in power. (6) Because of His resurrection, Jesus Christ reigns supreme. (7) Because of Jesus' resurrection, a Man is on the throne. (8) Because of Jesus' resurrection, believers have a new hope. (9) Because of Jesus' resurrection, future judgment is assured.

Lesson 12: Eternal Judgment

1. True, True, True
2. (1) According to truth, (2) According to deeds, (3) Without partiality, (4) According to the light available to those being judged
3. judgment, knee, tongue
4. (a) fire, (c) earth
5. (b) Because the Judge, Jesus, will reward you, not condemn you, while purifying you of your transgressions.

ABOUT THE AUTHOR

James W. Goll is the director of Encounters Network, based in Franklin, Tennessee, dedicated to changing lives and impacting nations by releasing God's presence through the prophetic, intercessory and compassion ministry. James is also the international director of Prayer Storm, a 24/7 media-based prayer ministry. He is also the director of the EN Alliance, a coalition of friends and God Encounters Training—E-School of the Heart. James has his B.S. in social work from Missouri State University and his doctorate in practical ministry from the Wagner Leadership Institute.

After pastoring in the Midwest, James was thrust into the role of itinerant ministry around the globe. He has traveled extensively across every continent carrying a passion for Jesus wherever he goes. James desires to see the Body of Christ come into maturity and become the house of prayer for all nations. He is the author of numerous books and training manuals as well as a contributing writer for several periodicals.

James is a founding instructor in the Wagner Leadership Institute and the Christian Leadership University. He is a member of the Harvest International Ministry Apostolic Team and a consultant to several regional, national and international ministries. James and Michal Ann Goll were married for over 32 years before her graduation to heaven in the fall of 2008. Their four adult children all love Jesus. James continues to make his home in the beautiful rolling hills of Franklin, Tennessee.

For More Information:

James W. Goll
Encounters Network
P.O. Box 1653
Franklin, TN 37065
office phone: 615-599-5552
email: info@encountersnetwork.com, or
info@prayerstorm.com
websites: www.encountersnetwork.com
www.prayerstorm.com
www.jamesgoll.com
www.compassionacts.com

Additional Resource Materials by James W. and Michal Ann Goll

The Lost Art of Intercession
God Encounters
Women on the Front Lines Series
Intercession
The Lost Art of Practicing His Presence
Praying for Israel's Destiny
The Coming Israel Awakening
The Beginner's Guide to Hearing God
The Coming Prophetic Revolution
The Call of the Elijah Revolution (with Lou Engle)
The Prophetic Intercessor
Shifting Shadows of Supernatural Experiences (with Julia Loren)
The Seer
The Seer 40-Day Devotional Journal
Prayer Storm
Prayer Storm Study Guide
The 365-Day Personal Prayer Guide
Empowered Prayer
Dream Language
Angelic Encounters
Discovering the Seer in You
Exploring the Nature and Gift of Dreams
Empowered Women
God's Supernatural Power in You (contributor)
Adventures in the Prophetic (contributor)
The Beginner's Guide to Signs, Wonders and the Supernatural Life
The Reformer's Pledge (contributor)
Deliverance from Darkness
Deliverance from Darkness Study Guide
The Lost Art of Pure Worship
Over twenty additional study guides
CD, MP3 and DVD albums